AMERICAN POLITICS
TODAY

Other books in the series

Political issues in America today
P. J. Davies and F. M. Waldstein

Political issues in Britain today
Bill Jones (editor)

British politics today
Bill Jones and P. J. Kavanagh

Trade unions in Britain today
J. McIlroy

West European politics today
G. K. Roberts and J. Lovecy

Irish politics today
N. Collins and F. McCann

Forthcoming, to include:

Parliament today
A. Adonis

General elections today
F. Conley

Government and the economy today
G. Thomas

Party politics today
R. N. Kelly and R. W. Garner

Soviet politics today
C. A. P. Binns

Local government today
J. A. Chandler

Of related interest

The financial system today
E. Rowley

AMERICAN
POLITICS TODAY

R. A Maidment and M. Tappin

Manchester University Press
Manchester and New York
Distributed exclusively in the USA and Canada by St. Martin's Press

This edition copyright © Richard Maidment and Michael Tappin 1989

First published 1982
Reprinted 1983 (with revisions), 1984
2nd edition 1985, reprinted 1987 and 1988 (with revisions)
by Manchester University Press
Oxford Road, Manchester M13 9PL, UK
and Room 400, 175 Fifth Avenue,
New York, NY 10010, USA

Distributed exclusively in the USA and Canada
by St. Martin's Press, Inc.,
175 Fifth Avenue, New York, NY 10010, USA

British Libarary calaloguing in publication data
Maidment, R.A. (Richard Anthony), *1944–*
  American politics today.– 3rd ed.
  1. United States. Politics
  I. Title   II. Tappin, M. (Michael)   III. Lees, John
  D. (John David), *1936–*. American politics today
  320.973

Library of Congress cataloging in publication data
Maidment, R. A. (Richard A.)
  American politics today / R. A. Maidment and M. Tappin.
    p.   cm.
  Reprint, with revisions. Originally published: Manchester, UK:
  ISBN 0–7190–3080–3 (U.S.). — ISBN 0–7190–3081–1 (pbk. : U.S.)
  1. United States—Politics and government.   I. Tappin, M.
  (Michael)   II. Title.
  JK31.L43   1989   89–38206
  320.973—dc20   CIP

ISBN 0 7190 3080 3 *hardback*
     0 7190 3081 1 *paperback*

Phototypeset in Great Britain
by Witwell Limited, Southport
Printed in Great Britain
by Biddles Ltd, Guildford and King's Lynn

CONTENTS

PREFACE

The first edition of *American Politics Today* appeared in 1982. At the time, the authors and the publishers were unsure of how the book would be received. It hardly needs to be said that we are very pleased that *American Politics Today* has not only survived but flourished in the very competitive market of politics textbooks. However, we take an even greater sense of satisfaction from the fact that both students and teachers of American politics and government, over the past seven years, have found this book useful. So when we began to plan the third edition, we resolved to maintain the format and style of the existing edition, but to update the chapters substantially. We wanted to maintain the objectives that we had established for the first edition, but to incorporate the many developments that have occurred in the political system of the United States since then. We hope that we have succeeded.

This edition, like its predecessors, sets out to provide students with an accessible introduction to the American political system. It is an extremely complex system, which requires a careful and gradual unravelling. We are aware from our own students that they are often surprised by the degree of complexity. They come to the study of American government with many preconceptions and somewhat fewer facts. Perhaps the most common assumption is that there is very little difference between the politics of the United States and that of Britain. Students are certainly more familiar with the United States, its music, literature and cinema, than with other 'foreign' societies, perhaps to the point that to be American no longer appears to be 'foreign'. But the United States is a very different society with a particular and distinctive history and political process. So this book does attempt to replace this and other preconceptions that students bring to the study of American government and politics, and replace them with a blend of insight and facts, description and analysis. While we have assumed that students have no knowledge of American politics prior to reading this book, we hope that by the time that they have finished it, they will have both an interest and an understanding of this most complex of political processes.

We have sought to preserve one of the most distinctive elements of the earlier editions of *American Politics Today*, which is to keep students informed of the most recent developments in the United States. Since the last edition there has been another presidential election, the Reagan era has ended, US/Soviet relations appared to have entered a new phase, the United States Supreme Court has a new Chief Justice – to mention a few, but perhaps the most significant developments. Accordingly, there is a new chapter on the 1988 elections and several of the other chapters have been modified substantially to take these developments into account.

There is, unfortunately, one change in the third edition that is most unwelcome. John Lees is no longer one of the authors of *American Politics Today*. He died unexpectedly in 1986 and his loss continues to be felt by his friends and colleagues. He was in the middle of a distinguished academic career with the promise of much more to come. We greatly valued his judgement and scholarship and were honoured to be his co-authors. We have attempted to ensure that this edition lives up to the very high standards that John set.

We would like to thank Alec McAulay, formerly of Manchester University Press, who encouraged us to write this book in 1982 and then ensured that we wrote the subsequent editions. We appreciate the assistance and the work of the staff of Manchester University Press in producing this edition. We are also very grateful to those people who have commented on this book through its various editions.

R. M
M. T.
Milton Keynes
January 1989

ABBREVIATIONS

ABA	American Bar Association
ABM Treaty	Anti-Ballistic Missiles Treaty
AFDC	Aid to Families with Dependent Children
AFL–CIO	American Federation of Labor—Congress of Industrial Organisations
AMA	American Medical Association
CBO	Congressional Budget Office
CEA	Council of Economic Advisers
CETA	Comprehensive Employment and Training Act (1974)
CIA	Central Intelligence Agency
CREEP	Committee to Re-elect the President
CRS	Congressional Research Service
DNC	Democratic National Committee
EPA	Environmental Protection Agency
FBI	Federal Bureau of Investigation
FEC	Federal Election Commission
FECA	Federal Election Campaign Act (1974)
GAO	General Accounting Office
INF Treaty	Intermediate Nuclear Forces Treaty
IRS	Internal Revenue Service
NAACP	National Association for the Advancement of Colored People
NAM	National Association of Manufacturers
NASA	National Aeronautics and Space Administration
NOW	National Organization for Women
NSC	National Security Council
OCDM	Office of Civil and Defense Mobilization
OMB	Office of Management and Budget
OPD	Office of Policy Development

OTA	Office of Technology Assessment
PAC	political action committee
PLO	Palestine Liberation Organization
RNC	Republican National Committee
SALT II	Second Strategic Arms Limitation Treaty

1

THE MAKING OF THE AMERICAN CONSTITUTION

On 4 July 1776 the American colonies issued a Declaration of Independence from Britain. The Declaration of Independence, written by Thomas Jefferson, set out the grievances that Americans felt towards the British government in general, and King George III in particular. Most Americans believed that these grievances were so serious that they were prepared to embark on a course of action which was extremely perilous. They were fully aware that Britain would resist American independence. They also realised that Britain was a great military power, and the war between Britain and America would be hard and bitter. So it proved until 1783, when Britain was forced to accept American independence. What then were the grievances that justified the risks and sacrifices? Why were Americans so confident that they were right in their conflict with Britain? Why did they believe that they would secure a better future as an independent country rather than as a British colony?

America in 1776

Most Americans in 1776, if insecure about their immediate future, were at least reasonably confident over the source of their problems and the way to deal with them. They believed that certain ideas or theories of politics and government offered them an analysis of, and a solution to, their predicament. What were these theories?

The theory of the Social Contract
Americans had a number of specific grievances with British rule, but underlying these specific complaints was a fundamental objection to the continuation of British rule. Most Americans no

longer accepted the right or legitimacy of Britain and its king to govern the American colonies. Why had King George III and his government lost this legitimacy? The answer is to be found in a theory of politics that was widely accepted in the American colonies: the theory of the Social Contract. The philosophers, the most famous of whom was the Englishman John Locke (1632–1704), who developed the notion of the Social Contract, claimed that the authority of a government to rule came from a contract which was made between all members of society when that society was first created. The ordinary individuals of that society agreed to give certain powers to the government, and to obey the laws and rules, if in return the government used these powers for the benefit of *all* the citizens. If the rulers abused these powers, then the Social Contract was void and the people no longer had any obligation to obey the government. In fact, wrote Thomas Jefferson in the Declaration of Independence, 'it is the right of the people to alter or abolish it [the existing government] and to institute a new government'. It is unsurprising that Americans found the idea of the Social Contract attractive. It provided them with an analysis that was very agreeable.

(*a*) The authority and legitimacy of governments came from the people.

(*b*) The powers that were granted to goverment were limited, and if these limited powers were abused then the people no longer had to obey their government.

(*c*) They also retained the right to rebel and overthrow the government.

The doctrine of separation of powers

In 1776 most Americans no longer accepted the right of the British government to rule the American colonies because they believed British rule to be tyrannical. They could point to specific instances of tyrannical behaviour, but they were also able to support their specific examples by citing a theory of government known as the doctrine of separation of powers. The doctrine of separation of powers that was expounded by the American colonists relied very heavily on the writings of a Frenchman, Baron Montesquieu (1689–1755). This doctrine of separation of powers, as developed by Montesquieu and others, provided the following analysis of government.

(*a*) There were three basic powers of government – an executive power, a legislative power and a judicial power.

(*b*) These three powers were distinct and should be separated.

(*c*) These powers should be exercised by three separate bodies or institutions.

(*d*) If these powers, however, were fused within one institution or person, such as a monarch, then tyranny could result. If any one body or institution exercised more than one of these powers, e.g., legislative and executive, there was a grave danger of a tyrannical government.

In the opinion of the American colonists, these three powers of government were not separated in Britain and consequently Britain had a tyrannical system of government.

So, in 1776, therefore, Americans felt that they were justified in their rebellion and that, after independence, they could create a system of government which would:

(*a*) be based on the consent of all citizens;

(*b*) avoid tyranny by using the principle of separation of powers;

(*c*) preserve liberty.

Despite the difficult and taxing war with Britian, Americans were confident of their cause, and optimistic of their ability to create a system of government that would avoid the pitfalls into which, they believed, the British had fallen.

From the Declaration of Independence to the American Constitution

The Convention which drafted the American Constitution met in Philadelphia in 1787. By then, a great deal of the confidence of 1776 had evaporated because of the events that had taken place during the previous eleven years. The most important developments during those years were:

1. The Confederation   In 1781 the thirteen American states entered into a Confederation. Because the individual states were primarily concerned with preserving their own sovereignty, and retaining their own powers, the institutions of the Confederation were relatively powerless. The Confederation Congress, the principal institution, did not have control over trade or the power to tax. It relied on the individual states to enforce its laws. The result was a system of government that was too weak and ineffective, and commanded no respect internally and abroad. For example, the British government refused to negotiate a treaty with the Confederation because it did not believe that the Confederation could enforce the treaty.

2. *The state constitutions* The constitutions of several state governments had used the principle of separation of powers. However, the behaviour of many of the state governments had also left a great deal to be desired. In 1776, the fear of tyranny, undoubtedly because of the behaviour of George III, centred on the misuse of the executive power. In the years after 1776, however, the state legislatures demonstrated that they could unfairly threaten the property and liberty of Americans. For instance, because of the economic depression that followed the end of the war with Britain, many people went into debt. They borrowed money, usually in the form of gold, but, when the repayments of these debts were due, they attempted to persuade the state legislatures to pass laws which would allow the repayment to be made in relatively valueless paper money. In other words, debtors would be paying back much less than they borrowed, and those who had lent the money were, in effect, having their money confiscated. Unfortunately, some legislatures went along with these proposals.

So in 1787 there was a very different mood in America. The national government for the previous six years had been ineffective. They now realised that any new national government system would have to be given specific powers and authority if it was to be effective. This did not mean that Americans had abandoned their belief that consent was required if government was to be legitimate, nor had they abandoned their commitment to liberty – it meant that Americans were now aware that the problem was more complex. There had to be a balance between governmental power on the one hand and the liberty of the individual on the other. Similarly, the idea that a government organised under the doctrine of separation of powers would not threaten personal liberty could no longer be accepted. This did not mean that the doctrine of separation of powers ought to be dispensed with, but it did need to be modified. The world of 1787 was far more complicated than that of 1776.

The Constitutional Convention of 1787

When the members of the Convention met, they realised that the task of creating a constitution was going to be very difficult. The members of the Convention represented different states and different interests. Inevitably there were going to be extended debates and arguments, and a constitution would only emerge if compromises were made. The Constitution that emerged did reflect the many compromises that were made in the Convention – but it would be true to say that the members of the Convention did share the same goals, even if there was disagreement on how to achieve those goals. So what were these objectives?

(a) *An effective national government.*
(b) *The protection of fundamental civil and political liberties.*

But the question remained, how were these objectives to be achieved?

The American Constitution

The Constitution that finally emerged from the Convention in Philadelphia created a dual system of government. There were individual state governments, and a national or federal government. The Convention preferred a *dual* or *federal* system to a unitary or single system because they feared the power of governments and wished to divide the responsibilities of government into a number of separate components. The federal or national government was given specific powers and responsibilities to deal with those problems facing the American nation, for example, foreign affairs and trade. The remaining responsibilities and duties of government were reserved to the individual state governments. This desire to contain and limit the powers and responsibilities of government can also be seen in the structure of the federal system.

The federal government

The federal government was designed to give the United States an effective national government. It was also designed to ensure that the institutions of the national government did not abuse the powers which they have been given. The principal institutions of the federal government are:

(a) *The presidency*, which embodies the executive power.

(b) *The Congress*, the legislature, which is composed of an upper house, the *Senate*, and a lower house, the *House of Representatives*.

(c) *The courts*, which incorporate the judicial power. The *United States Supreme Court* is the final court of appeal.

All these institutions were given specific powers to fulfil those duties and responsibilities which were set out in the Constitution. However, to ensure that these powers would not be abused, the Convention attempted to make these three institutions rivals for power. The Convention wished each of these institutions to *check and balance* each other. Deliberate points of tension were created, which would increase the antagonism between the institutions.

(a) The President was appointed Commander-in-Chief of the armed forces – *but* only Congress could declare war.

(b) The President was given the power of veto over legislation passed by the Congress – *But* the veto could be overriden if there was a two-thirds majority in both the Senate and the House of Representatives.

(c) The President was given the power of appointment of ambassadors, government officials, etc. – *but* the appointments had to be confirmed by the Senate.

(d) The President was given the power to make treaties – *but* the treaty had to be approved by a two-thirds majority of the Senate.

(e) The courts had the potential power of judicial review: that is, the potential to declare the actions of both Congress and President unconstitutional.

The Convention hoped that these points of friction would prevent any one institution from gaining too much power, because the other institutions would be too jealous of their own position to let it happen. It was the genius of the American Constitution to ally the idea of checks and balances to the doctrine of separation of powers. The Convention hoped that this would prevent the abuse of power by either the executive or legislative branches of government.

1. The presidency   The Constitutional Convention was uncertain about the presidency. There were longer and passionate debates about the office. Should the President be elected for four years or eight years? Should he be re-electable? Beware of making him too powerful, said some, while others feared that the President might become a mere figurehead. Eventually, after many compromises, the office emerged from the Convention. Because of these compromises every member of the Convention did not agree with every aspect of the presidential office. Nevertheless, there was, in the end, a wide measure of agreement that the Constitution had got the balance right. What were the main features of the presidency set out in Article II of the Constitution?

(*a*) The presidency was given specific powers, in order to be an effective office and to resist any encroachment from the Congress (see Chapter 5).

(*b*) Nevertheless, precautions were taken to ensure that the powers of the President would not be abused (see above).

(*c*) The presidency was seen as an institution which would provide caution and restraint and oppose the more radical tendencies of the Congress.

(*d*) The method of election would ensure that the President would be protected, to a certain extent, from public opinion, so that he could consider the lasting national interest rather than temporary changes in the political mood.

So what are the procedures for electing a President?

(*a*) *A President is elected for a term of four years.*

(*b*) *He is re-electable.* Initially Presidents were re-electable for an indefinite number of terms. Only one President was re-elected more than twice, Franklin Rosoevelt (1933–45). Indeed, because Roosevelt was elected on four occasions, the Twenty-second Amendment to the Constitution was adopted in 1951, prohibiting any person from being elected more than twice.

(*c*) *The President is elected by an electoral college.* He is not directly elected by the people. To be elected, a candidate for the presidency must gain a majority of the electoral college vote –

he does not need a majority of the popular vote – and there have been instances such as in 1888 when a candidate has received fewer popular votes than his opponent, but nevertheless gained a majority of electoral college votes.

(*d*) *The electoral college is composed of representatives from each state*. Each state is allocated a number of electoral votes which is equal to the state's representation in the Congress. So if a state has three members in the House of Representatives, plus two in the Senate, it will have five electoral college votes. Currently there are 538 electoral college votes.

(*e*) *In 1787 the state representatives to the electoral college were chosen by the state legislatures*. Currently they are elected directly by the public.

(*f*) *There were two 'buffers' between the President and the electorate* because the President was elected by an electoral college, which in turn was chosen by the state legislatures. Therefore, he had the political room and ability to ignore public pressures. The Convention hoped that, because he was 'distanced' from public opinion, the President would take a more sensible and long-term view and would not be swayed by a temporary whim or fashion. The Congress, and in particular the House of Representatives, would express the current and immediate feelings; the President, it was hoped, would provide a balance.

(*g*) *The President is the only official to be elected by a 'national' constituency*. Again, this provides a contrast to both the Senate and the House of Representatives. Undoubtedly the difference in the constituencies would cause a degree of friction between the various institutions.

2. The vice-presidency   The vice-presidency was not particularly well defined in the Constitution. The Vice-President was principally a replacement for the President in the event of his death, resignation or removal from office. No further thoughts appear to have been given to the office. Consequently, the vice-presidency became a largely ceremonial office, and was described by a former Vice-President as not being worth 'a pitcher of warm spit'. However, in recent years, there have been attempts to give the Vice-President a greater role in the affairs of government. Certainly under Jimmy Carter, Vice-President Walter Mondale played a significant role in the making of public policy. The Vice-

President is also elected by the electoral college. Initially, under the Constitution, the candidate elected Vice-President was the person who received the second largest number of electoral college votes. However, in 1804 the Twelfth Amendement was adopted, which separated the elections for President and Vice-President.

3. The Congress   The Convention deliberately chose to have a *bicameral* legislature – a legislature composed of two houses. The Convention, in Article I, chose to create two houses because it saw each fulfilling a rather different role. Therefore it gave them different powers (see Chapter 6). The Convention gave them different constituencies and a different election procedure.

(*a*) **The House of Representatives** was seen by the Convention as the radical or dynamic institution of the federal government, because it was *elected directly* by the people. Furthermore, elections to the House of Representatives took place every *two* years for all members of the House. Therefore, the members of the House were expected to know and represent the interests of the general public.

(*b*) *Each state was allocated representation in the House on a population basis.* The larger the population of a state the greater its representation in the House. Currently there are 435 members in the House of Representatives.

(*c*) *If a state has more than one member* of the House of Representatives – and most states do – then the state is divided into constituencies of roughly equal population size. The House therefore represents interests within states.

(*d*) **The Senate**, by contrast, was seen as a conservative counterweight to the more populist House of Representatives. Senators are elected every six years – but the elections to the Senate are staggered so that one-third of the Senate is elected every two years. In 1787, the Senate was elected by the state legislatures. However, in 1913, the Seventeenth Amendment to the Constitution was adopted, which required the direct election, by the electorate, of the Senate. Clearly the six-year term and the indirect election to the Senate was intended to provide the Senators some insulation of protection from public opinion.

(*e*) *The Senate represents the states.* Each state, regardless of population, has two Senators. The Senate, therefore, was organised on a territorial basis. Currently there are 100 Senators.

(f) *The intentions of the Constitutional Convention concerning the Congress are clear*. They sought to create tension and antagonism between the House and Senate just as they had sought to do between the President and Congress. They used the same devices of different constituencies, different election procedures and different interests to ensure this hostility.

4. The courts   There is a degree of uncertainty over the Constitutional Convention's intentions concerning the courts. Under Article III a court system was created, with the United States Supreme Court as the final court of appeal. However, although the Constitution does deal with certain aspects of jurisdiction, it does not explicitly give the courts the power of *judicial review* – the power to decide whether actions of the President, Congress or state governments violate the American Constitution (see Chapter 4). However, despite the Constitution's ambiguity on this subject, the courts took on the duty and play an important role in the system of checks and balances. If the President, the Senate and the House of Representatives do not succeed in controlling each other sufficiently, the courts have the authority to declare their actions constitutionally invalid.

The state governments
The American Constitution is overwhelmingly concerned with the powers, duties and responsibilities of the federal government. There is relatively little in the Constitution about the state governments. Article IV refers to certain aspects of the responsibilities and duties of the states. Article I Section X deals with restrictions on the states. The Tenth Amendment to the Constitution, which was adopted in 1791, does say that those powers not specifically delegated to the federal government are reserved for the states.

The process of constitutional amendment
The Constitutional Convention intended the American Constitution to endure. It did not wish the Constitution to be tampered with; however, the Convention recognised that the

Constitution could need amending to meet changes and developments. Article V sets out the procedures to amend the Constitution. There are two alternntive procedures, but the one that has been primarily used requires an amendment to be passed by a two-thirds majority in both houses of Congress and ratified by three-quarters of the state legislatures. The amendment procedures have been used successfully on only twenty-six occasions.

The protection of civil liberties

The Constitution of 1787 did not include specific references to political and civil liberties. In 1791 ten amendments to the Constitution were adopted, which together are known as the Bill of Rights and which guarantee certain political and civil liberties. The most important aspects of the Bill of Rights are:

(a) *The First Amendment* guarantees freedom of religion, speech and press.

(b) *The Fourth Amendment* prohibits unreasonable searches and seizures of persons and their effects by government.

(c) *The Fifth Amendment* protects a person's right not to incriminate himself in criminal proceedings.

(d) *The Sixth Amendment* guarantees the accused, in a criminal prosecution, the right to have a lawyer.

(e) *The Eighth Amendment* prohibits cruel and unusual punishments.

Summary

The Constitutional Convention attempted to create a system of government which would:

(a) provide an effective national government;
(b) ensure the liberties of Americans.

In order to achieve these objectives the Constitution was based on:

(a) the doctrine of separation of powers;
(b) the idea of checks and balances;
(c) government institutions of limited and specific powers;
(d) constitutional guarantees of political and civil liberties.

Further reading

M. J. Heale, *The Making of American Politics*, Longman, 1977.

A. H. Kelly and W. A. Harbison, *The American Constitution: Its Origins and Development*, W. W. Norton, 1970.

Richard Maidment and John Zvesper (eds.), *Reflections on the Constitution: The American Constitution after Two Hundred Years*, Manchester University Press, 1989.

J. W. Peltason, *Understanding the Constitution*, 8th edn, Holt, Rinehart and Winston, 1979.

C. L. Rossiter, *1787, The Grand Convention*, MacGibbon & Kee, 1968.

Questions

1. What were the principal objectives of the Constitutional Convention?

2. Has the idea of checks and balances been effective?

THE AMERICAN POLITICAL TRADITION

The United States takes pride in its diversity. It has attracted and continues to attract immigrants from a wide variety of racial, religious, ethnic and socio-economic backgrounds. This diversity is seen in the Constitution, and in the political and other traditions of the society. Throughout its history, political theories and ideas representing an enormous range of opinion have been articulated and represented in the United States. There have been anarchist, conservative, Marxist and socialist movements, amongst many others. So in one sense diversity of opinion itself is an established American political tradition. However, anarchism or socialism, to name but two, have generally been peripheral to the American experience; rightly or wrongly, most Americans have found them irrelevant. The political beliefs and values that have been most relevant and central to the American experience are those of *constitutional liberal democracy*.

Liberal democratic ideas have been dominant in America and have had the greatest impact on Americans, so we should examine these beliefs. But before doing this we should consider why it is of particular importance to talk about political ideas in relation to the study of American politics and government.

The relationship between political ideas and political behaviour

The nature of the relationship between ideas and beliefs on the one hand and political behaviour on the other will be evident if we take as an example racial discrimination. Clearly many ethnic minorities in America, particularly blacks, have been and continue to be subjected to discrimination. Yet discrimination, despite its persistence, is a practice that is very difficult to justify in America. Only those on the fringes of American politics have advocated or do advocate racial discrimination as a policy. Why is this so? The answer is that it is impossible to advocate racial discrimination without violating certain beliefs central to liberal democratic values. A key liberal belief concerns the importance of the individual (see below). An individual must be judged only by his or her personal or instrinsic qualities. If an individual is judged by other criteria, such as race or class – if he or she is treated only as a representative of a race or class, rather than as a person in his or her own right – then his or her individuality is denied. It is hard to imagine a more fundamental violation of liberal democratic beliefs.

Consequently, those who wanted to subordinate black Americans had to devise a series of ploys to achieve their objective without actually advocating racial discrimination. For instance, in several Southern states the right to vote, until 1965, was dependent on passing literacy test. Unsurprisingly, it was usually blacks who were judged to have failed such a test! There are many other examples of such devices.

The important point, therefore, is that liberal democratic ideas and beliefs have had and continue to have an impact on political behaviour. Obviously these ideas and beliefs can be and are violated, but they do affect what is said and done and how it is said and done.

The beliefs of American liberal democracy

Over the past two hundred years the values and beliefs of liberal democracy have not remained constant. They have adapted to the changing circumstances of American society. However, certain ideas have remained central. Here are three of the most important.

1. Individualism   The liberal view of society is that it exists for the benefit of the individual members of that society. Indeed, a society is formed only to provide the individual citizen with the liberty to pursue his or her own happiness (see discussion of the Declaration of Independence in Chapter 1). If a society does not achieve this objective, it has failed and the individual no longer has an obligation to obey the laws of the society. The individual and his liberty and freedom to achieve and to develop his or her own life is at the centre of the values of American liberty democracy. Consequently, Americans have always seen their country as a land of individual opportunity, from the settler who tamed the wilderness to the men like Andrew Jackson in the 1820s or Abraham Lincoln in 1860, who came from a log cabin to occupy the White House as President. The story of personal achievement against the odds, regardless of background, or to put it another way from rags to riches, has always been celebrated in America.

2. Civil liberties   If an individual is to fulfil his or her potential, then his or her liberty and freedom must be protected. Americans have always believed that the greatest threat to that liberty and freedom comes from government. The Watergate affair in the early 1970s (see Chapter 5) confirmed this view. Consequently, the civil liberties of Americans were guaranteed by the first ten amendments to Constitution and, over the past two hundred years, have been protected by the Supreme Court (see Chapters 1 and 4). As a result American citizens enjoy a greater degree of protection from governmental abuse of their civil liberties than the citizens of virtually any other country. Nevertheless, it is worth remembering that despite these protections, and the importance placed on civil liberties in American society, there have been several episodes when the civil liberties of American citizens have been abused. For example, there were the 'red scares' after both world wars, when the civil liberties of many Americans were violated by the zeal of politicians and government officials seeking to uncover communist subversion in the United States.

3. Private property   From the outset American society has stressed the importance of the ownership of property. By 1776, Americans believed that the liberty to own and to acquire property was as important as any other civil liberty, such as freedom of speech or religion. Therefore property rights were protected in the Fifth and Fourteenth Amendments to the Constitution, and the Supreme Court throughout the nineteenth and early twentieth centuries was very careful to ensure that property rights were not infringed. Perhaps by the middle of the twentieth century, property rights were no longer considered as significant as the freedom of speech and religion, but nevertheless they continue to be an important and widely held value.

There are, of course, many other constituents of American liberal democratic beliefs, such as the supremacy of the law, i.e., that the United States is a nation governed by law not men. Most have changed considerably over time. For instance, there were great worries about majority rule when the Constitution was being written, but these had by and large disappeared by the twentieth century. Of course, some of the procedures and institutions of American government still reflect those eighteenth-century fears: for example, the check imposed by the Senate on the House of Representatives, or the need for two-thirds majority support in both houses of Congress for constitutional amendments. However, no politician today in the age of universal suffrage can worry, in public at least, about the dangers of majority rule. There are several other examples of values adapting the changing circumstances. Still there remains a core of values which have remained constant and which continue to influence political life at all levels in the United States.

Further reading

R. Hofstadter, *The American Political Tradition*, Vintage, 1958.

Questions

1. What are the central features of the American liberal tradition?

3

FEDERALISM

The principle of federalism, as seen in Chapter 1, was made an important feature of the American Constitution by the members of the Constitutional Convention of 1787. Today it may appear, at first glance, to be one of the less important or even less in teresting aspects of American government. First impressions, however, could well be misleading. Federalism has excited passions in the past and was one of the most divisive of political issues in the early years of the American Republic. Indeed, it was one of the factors that led to the secession of the Southern states: a secession that culminated in the American Civil War and the loss of the lives of almost half a million men. In the aftermath of the Civil War, which reaffirmed the authority of the national government in Washington, there was still a lively debate about the relationship between the federal government and that of the individual states. Although the precise details of the debate have changed during the twentieth century, the relationship between the states and Washington is still a subject of controversy. In recent years, the Reagan administration, most notably, wanted to modify the nature of this relationship. So federalism has and continues to play an integral and important part in American political life.

The changing nature of federalism (1787–1945)

Federalism and the Constitution
As we have seen in Chapter 1, the members of the Constitutional Convention in 1787 shared certain broad objectives but were unsure over how to achieve them. Federalism was one of the devices which they hoped would provide effective government without endangering the political liberty of Americans. Accord-

ingly, the Constitution established a strong national government and gave it the sole responsibility for conducting the foreign affairs of the United States, the issuing of a national currency, promoting the general welfare and the provision for a national defence, amongst its other reponsibilities. The Constitution also provided this new government with the powers to fulfil these responsibilities. However, because they were concerned that the powers of the federal government were also a potential source of danger to the liberties of American citizens, the members of the Convention also took great pains to ensure that the states had a very important role to play within the new Constitution. The powers of the federal government were specific and limited. All powers that were not enumerated in the Constitution were 'reserved to the States respectively, or to the people' (the Tenth Amendment). The states are therefore responsible for all those areas of governmental activity which are not specifically allocated to the federal government. For instance, the states can levy their own rates of taxation, create their own criminal code, organise their educational system. In other words, many of the areas of public life that most affect the ordinary citizens come within the jurisdiction of the states. Clearly, the framers of the American Constitution believed that the states had a very critical and important role to play. They sought to create two distinct arenas of governmental activity, one at the state level and the other at the national level. This then was the federal relationship as the framers of the Constitution conceived it.

The federal relationship in the early nineteenth century
Despite the framers' intentions there was a considerable degree of uncertainty over boundaries between the powers of the states and that of the national government. For instance, a state government had the power to regulate intra-state commerce, that is the commercial activities that took place within the boundaries of that state. However, the federal government had the authority to regulate interstate commerce, the commercial transactions that crossed state boundaries. While this distinction was very clear to the framers of the Constitution, because the economy in 1787 was overwhelmingly rural and agrarian, it became progressively less so. As the economy became more sophisticated, interdependent and less local in outlook, this distinction between inter- and intra-states was more difficult to divine. The courts had to adjudicate

this dispute and other similar disputes between national and state power, and in the early nineteenth century the Supreme Court was far more sympathetic to the claims of the federal government. In cases like *McCulloch* v. *Maryland* (1819) and *Gibbons* v. *Ogden* (1824) (see Chapter 4), the Court expanded the authority of the national government and diminished that of the states. The pendulum in the federal relationship swung towards the national government.

Dual federalism

The pendulum swung back, however, in the years before the Civil War. Again it was the Supreme Court that defined the federal relationship. But during this period leading up to the Civil War, the Court interpreted the Constitution to mean that it had created a system where the national government and the governments of the states had separate grants of power, with each supreme in its own sphere. In this interpretation of the federal relationship, known as dual federalism, the two levels of government are equal. The differences between them are those of jurisdictions and not of inequalities. It was during this period that those who championed the powers of the states were going even further and arguing that the states could nullify a federal law or could even secede from the Union. Of course, the triumph of the Northern States in the Civil War ended the calls for secession and the doctrine of nullification, but the doctrine of dual federalism had some considerable life in it.

From the Civil War to the New Deal

In the aftermath of the Civil War, the Supreme Court continued to define the federal relationship broadly in terms of dual federalism. However, the very rapid developments that were taking place in both the American economy and in the society at large meant that there were many attempts to expand the role and activities of the federal government. In particular, legislation was passed to abolish child labour and regulate the hours that women could work. However, the Supreme Court in this period was reluctant to permit a very substantial expansion in the powers of the federal government. It was not persuaded that the conditions of an industrial society justified altering in any fundamental manner the federal relationship that existed. Between 1874 and

1937 the Supreme Court found fifty federal laws unconstitutional, laws which mainly sought to expand the role of the national government. The result was that by the early twentieth century the United States had a national government that intervened far less in economic and social arrangements than in other comparable societies.

The New Deal

The New Deal was a watershed for the federal relationship, as it was for so many other aspects of American politics and government. The Great Depression, which started with the Wall Street Crash in 1929, devastated American society. The scale of economic hardship and dislocation overwhelmed the state governments; they could not deal with the problems that the economic depression brought in its train. As a consequence the electorate looked to the federal government and the new administration of President Franklin D. Roosevelt (1933–45) to cope with the depression. The administration took up the challenge and passed a series of Acts, known collectively as the New Deal, which brushed aside the traditional understandings of the role of the federal government. Under the New Deal, the federal government intervened in the economy as it had never done so in the past. It regulated, amongst other activities, working conditions and labour practices, which it had not been allowed to do so in the past and which had previously been designated as being within the province of the states. The Supreme Court initially refused to endorse the constitutionality of this legislation (see Chapter 4), but finally the Court came to accept that such federal intervention was constitutional in the conditions that prevailed in a modern industrial economy. The New Deal fundamentally altered the relationship between the federal government and the states. One indication of the substantial change in the role of the federal government can be seen in the very striking changes that occurred in the figures for governmental expenditure, excluding defence spending, between 1929 and 1939. The federal government share of this expenditure in 1929 was 17 per cent but by 1939 it was 47 per cent. Dual federalism was dead and the national government was firmly in the ascendant. The federal relationship changed irrevocably with the New Deal and has not been quite the same since then.

The federal relationship in modern America (1945–   )

The years since 1945 have seen a constant increase in the expansion of the federal government's activities. Even Presidents who were hostile to 'big' government and had campaigned against the Washington bureaucracy have nevertheless presided over new programmes and further expansion of the federal government. The Republican administration of President Richard M. Nixon (1969–74) offers a particularly good example of this phenomenon. Of course, the Democrats who embraced the notion of big government with the New Deal and continued to do so until the 1970s when disenchantment set in, also increased the activities of the national government and no one did more to do so than President Lyndon B. Johnson (1963–69). The Johnson administration was responsible for the Great Society legislative programme, which perhaps created the most substantial expansion of federal activities, in almost every area imaginable, of any administration. Since 1945 federal involvement has been introduced into such areas as education (primary, secondary and pre-school), mass transit, highway construction and many others, several of which until then had been assumed to be within the province of the states and the localities. But interestingly, while there has been this almost inexorable increase in the size and activities of the federal government, there have also been several attempts to rethink the federal relationship.

The starting point for this rethinking of the relationship was a growing sense that the federal government has become too big, too bureaucratic and too remote from the American population. Washington was too far away to know, with any precision, the desires and the needs of a very heterogeneous population. That which was wanted and requested in Louisiana, might not be appropriate for Minnesota. It was far more likely that institutions and politicians closer to the electorate would have a far better idea of what was needed and desired by the electorate, which of course was one of the most important reasons for the initial creation of a federal structure. The only difficulty with reinstating a federal relationship that the framers of the Constitution might have recognised was that the states, or the localities, did not have the necessary financial resources. The federal government did; it was relatively rich, although its resources were and are not unlimited (see Chapter 10). But even so, according to two observers, 'affluence lies with the national government, while the effluents (sewage) are the responsibility of the states and cities'. So most of the proposals over the past decades have tried to harness local knowledge, interest and dynamism to federal money, which has been disbursed through federal grants, primarily to the states. The following are the most notable of these reworkings of the federal relationship.

Creative federalism

This was very much an initiative of the Great Society years (1963–69), whereby links were forged between the federal government and governmental authorities, especially those in urban areas. Some of the most striking of the Great Society Programmes, such as the Economic Opportunity Act of 1964 and the Demonstration Cities and Metropolitan Development Act of 1966, sought to ally the expertise and energy of the local institutions and people to federal grants in order to deal with the problems of poverty and urban renewal. These programmes were devised with the intention that the ideas and proposals should emerge from the local communities and that the federal government would provide the funds. There would not be the usual list of bureaucratic criteria and controls that normally accompanied federal grants. In order to further encourage the process, the states were bypassed. In this respect creative federalism was particularly distinctive because in many instances the federal government ignored the states and went directly to the localities. Until the Great Society programmes, most federal grants went either directly to the states or were channelled through the states to local governments. However, creative federalism cannot be counted a success, certainly not a political success. Several of the programmes foundered on the political hostility of those institutions and politicians who were ignored.

New federalism

This was the name given by President Nixon to his proposed rearrangement of federal/state relations. Again the idea behind it was to give the states and the localities a greater say in the spending of federal grants. The difference between the new federalism and that which went before was the notion of general revenue sharing. Essentially general revenue sharing provided federal money with very few strings attached. Nixon initially proposed this in 1969, but did not obtain Congressional approval until 1972, when $30 billion as allocated to general revenue sharing over a period of five years. The programme was relatively popular, although there was some opposition in Congress to their loss of control over federal money. Interestingly, in 1980 the legislation was amended to exclude states from revenue sharing and it became a federal/local programme entirely.

Another feature of the federal relationship in the Nixon administration was the introduction of the federal block grant. Block grants were a compromise between the very substantial restrictions and controls that Congress normally imposed on federal aid, and the almost unlimited discretion of revenue sharing. Block Grants allowed the administration and the Congress to establish broad objectives, while still allowing states and local governments a considerable discretion in the spending of the money. A good example of the block grant system was the Comprehensive Employment and Training Act (CETA) of 1974, designed to alleviate unemployment.

Reagan's new federalism

In his inaugural address, President Reagan declared that it was his 'intention to curb the size of influence of the federal establishment and to demand recognition of the distinction between the powers granted to the federal government and those reserved to the states and the people'. In order to fulfil this belief that the federal government had become too large and powerful at the expense of the states, President Reagan sought to restructure many federal aid programmes to the states. He wanted to diminish federal assistance and give back to the states a greater degree of control over a host of programmes. Interestingly his proposals were not welcomed by state governors or city mayors. They were not welcomed because, along with greater control, the Reagan proposals were also handing back to the states and the cities a far greater financial responsibility which they did not want. Accordingly, most of the Reagan proposals were defeated in the Congress, although the Reagan administration did have a modest success in reducing the overall level of federal aid to the states and localities, especially in 1981. Subsequent attempts to further lower federal aid foundered on considerable hostility within the Congress and in the states and cities. The opposition to the Reagan notion that the states and localities should only spend what they could raise in their own taxes was based on the realisation that either tax rates would have to be increased dramatically or existing programmes, dependent on federal grants, would have to be ended. Neither alternative was politically acceptable, even in the conditions of the 1980s when public resources were under pressure. The Reagan conception of a modern dual federalism was not politically viable. The role of the federal government could not be withdrawn to the extent that the President had wished in 1981, and by the time that he left office he had to come to accept this fact of modern American political life. President Bush has given every indication that he is not going to attempt to rewrite the modern federal relationship.

Further reading

Richard Maidment and John Zvesper (eds.), *Reflections on the Constitution: The American Constitution After Two Hundred Years*, Manchester University Press, 1989.

Michael D. Reagan and John G. Sanzone, *The New Federalism*, Oxford University Press, 1981.

M. J. C. Vile, *The Structure of American Federalism*, Oxford University Press, 1961.

Questions

1. Describe and analyse the principal changes in the federal relationship during the twentieth century.

4

THE SUPREME COURT AND THE JUDICIAL PROCESS

Over the past two hundred years, the United States Supreme Court has attempted to interpret the American Constitution. The Supreme Court's judgements have been satisfactory to some Americans, while even those who were less than happy with the Court's judgements have nevertheless accepted the authority of the Court to interpret the Constitution. Admittedly on some occasions the Court's decisions have aroused widespread hostility and there have been attempts to amend the Constitution. However, the amendment procedure has been used successfully a mere twenty-six times, and only a very few of these amendments were intended to nullify a Court decision. Thus the Supreme Court, in effect, does have the last word on constitutional matters, and it is this fact which gives the United States Supreme Court enormous influence within the American system of government.

The Supreme Court is the final arbiter of whether an act of Congress, a presidential executive order or legislation passed by any of the fifty state governments, is constitutionally permissible. The Court, since 1787, has exercised this authority on many occasions and declared presidential actions and federal and state legislation unconstitutional. Clearly then, the Supreme Court's decisions, on the constitutionality of laws in particular, have a very substantial impact on American society and politics. Therefore, it is crucial for students of American government and politics to understand how this judicial institution works. Where does the Court derive its authority to interpret the American Constitution? On what basis do the justices of the Supreme Court make their decisions? What are the criteria for appointing a Supreme Court justice? Is the Court a political or judicial body? This chapter will attempt to provide an answer to these and other questions.

The Court and the Constitution

The powers of the courts in general and the Supreme Court in particular are set out in Article III of the Constitution (see p. 199). The Constitution establishes certain elements of the judicial system very clearly.

(a) *The judicial power of the United States is vested in the Supreme Court and in such inferior courts that the Congress may decide to establish* (Article III Section I). The Constitution does not permit the Congress the opportunity to create a rival judicial system if it does not happen to approve of the decisions of the Supreme Court.

(b) *Judges, both of the Supreme Court and lower courts, shall retain their office during good behaviour* and their salaries cannot be reduced after their appointment (Article III Section I). The framers of the Constitution clearly did not wish the judiciary to be vulnerable to financial pressure or threats of removal.

(c) *The courts have the power to consider all cases in all and equity arising from the Constitution, the laws of the United States, treaties, etc.* (Article III Section II). The Constitution gives the courts jurisdiction over virtually all litigation concerning constitutional, federal and international law, but it does require the courts to deal with specific cases arising out of litigation. The Supreme Court cannot issue advisory opinions on matters of national importance; it can only decide those questions brought before it through the process of litigation.

(d) *The Supreme Court is established as an appeals court*, although there is a small category of cases where it is a court of original jurisdiction (Article III Section II).

(e) *Supreme Court judges are nominated by the President*, and their nomination must be approved by the Senate (Article II Section II).

The Constitution is not clear on certain other matters:

(a) *The number of judges on the Supreme Court.* The current number of Supreme Court judges is nine. For most of the twentieth century the Court has had nine justices, but there is nothing sacrosanct about this figure. The Congress has the power, and has used it in the past, to increase or decrease the number of judges.

(*b*) *The Constitution does not explicitly give the Supreme Court the task of being the final constitutional arbiter*. It does not say that the Court has authority to evaluate, for example, the constitutionality of an act of Congress. The Constitution does not give explicitly to the Courts the power of judicial review.

Judicial review

If the Constitution did not explicitly give the judiciary the power to review the action of the other branches of the federal government and the state governments, why then did the practice of judicial review take root? There are two principal reasons:

1. The concept of judicial review fits in fairly easily with the philosophical beliefs that lay behind the American Constitution (see Chapter 1). The Constitution clearly reflects the distrust – expressed in a variety of devices – that Americans in the eighteenth century felt towards politicians and indeed the activity of politics itself. Judicial review was another manifestation of this distrust. The Constitution was seen by the framers as the fundamental law of the United States and its integrity had to be protected. Which institution should provide this protection? The answer, to many Americans, was obvious. The political branches of government, e.g., the Congress or the presidency, were susceptible to factional pressures and consequently were not entirely reliable. Courts and judges, on the other hand, were far more likely to protect the Constitution, as they were distanced from the political process. It must be emphasised, however, that this view was widely expressed and drew considerable support at the time the Constitution was being drawn up and ratified; but it was a view which was not held unanimously, and many leading political figures at the time vehemently disagreed with the notion of judicial review.

2. The leadership of John Marshall John Marshall was the Chief Justice of the United States Supreme Court from 1801 to 1835. The Court, in the first decade and a half of its existence, was an unsure and insecure institution. It lived in the shadow of the Congress and the presidency, but under Marshall the Court became far more assertive and established the practice of judicial review, and through judicial review its influence on American society and politics. Marshall's talent as a judicial statesman has been described as 'pre-eminent – first with no one second'. Perhaps one case, which is the single most important case in establishing the practice of judical review, *Marbury* v. *Madison* (1803), best illustrates Marshall's skill and intelligence.

Marbury v. ***Madison (1803)***   The facts in this case emerge from the political rivalry that occurs when one President leaves office and the incoming President is a political opponent. In the final hours of his administration, President John Adams made a series of 'midnight' appointments to various offices in order to prevent these positions from being filled by the new President, Thomas Jefferson. The commission of one of these appointments, William Marbury, was signed and sealed, but it was not delivered to Marbury, and Jefferson was not willing to rectify this oversight. Marbury thereupon went to court in order to compel James Madison, Jefferson's Secretary of State, to hand over the commission. The problem facing the Supreme Court was immensely difficult. The situation was fraught with danger for the Court. If the Court dismissed Marbury's claim, it would appear impotent and frightened of offending the President. However, if it ordered Madison to deliver the commission and he refused, then the Court's credibility and effectiveness could be permanently destroyed. It must also be remembered that the Jefferson administration was suspicious of the Court in general and Marshall in particular, as he was known to be unsympathetic to Jefferson and his party. However, Chief Justice Marshall, who wrote the opinion of the Court, was aware of the judicial and political minefields and managed to avoid them, which is an indication of his immense talent. His opinion can be summarised in the following manner:

(*a*) Marbury's commission was being illegally withheld.

(*b*) However, the Supreme Court was not the proper body to provide redress, because the Judiciary Act of 1789, which gave the Supreme Court the authority to provide redress, was itself unconstitutional, according to Marshall.

(*c*) Marbury must therefore look elsewhere for a resolution to his problem.

Therefore Marshall had asserted the right of the Supreme

Court to review, in *Marbury* v. *Madison*, an action of the President and an Act of Congress, but because the Jefferson administration had in a sense won the case, they did not challenge Marshall's judgement. Judicial review was established, almost by stealth.

The Supreme Court in the nineteenth and early twentieth centuries

The Marshall Court
Opponents of judicial review did not disappear after *Marbury* v. *Madison*, but by the time Marshall died in 1835 the Court's authority and power was a fact of political life. In two cases, *Fletcher* v. *Peck* (1810) and *Cohens* v. *Virginia* (1812), the Court returned to the question of judicial review and reasserted the superiority of the judiciary in constitutional interpretation over the other branches of government, both federal and state. The other major achievement of the Marshall Court was to emphasise the importance of the nation as opposed to the individual states: to strengthen the powers of the federal government at the expense of the state governments. In this respect the most significant cases were *McCulloch* v. *Maryland* (1819) and *Gibbons* v. *Ogden* (1824). Both of these decisions increased the federal government's control over the economy.

The Taney Court
When Marshall died he was replaced by Roger B. Taney, a choice which did not please the friends and supporters of Marshall. They feared that Taney was a radical who would not assert the power of the judiciary and would not protect property rights. However, this did not transpire. There was no break with the decisions of the Marshall Court, and this helped the authority of the Court. The continuity increased the sense of judicial impartiality which defused criticism of the Court, and for a period in the 1840s there was an era of judicial good feeling. However, this good feeling dissipated when the contentious issue of slavery came before the Court. The Court, whatever it did, was likely to offend either the Northern states or the slave-owning states of the South. In 1857 the Court considered the case of Dred Scott. Scott was a slave, who had been taken into an area which was designated to be free of slavery under the Missouri Compromise. Scott sued his owner

in court, claiming that, as he was in a free area, he was a free man. The opinion of the Supreme Court was written by Chief Justice Taney. He declared that only a citizen could bring a suit in court, but as Scott was a Negro, and Negroes were not citizens, Scott was not entitled to bring a suit. Furthermore, Taney ruled that the Missouri Compromise itself was unconstitutional. The Chief Justice's opinion was, and still is, seen as disastrous. He was vilified and abused by the Northern press and politicians, and the Court lost a great deal of respect and trust. *Dred Scott* v. *Sandford* (1857), however, is indicative of the enormous impact a Court decision can have on American society and politics.

The post-Civil War Court

The Court in this period was not dominated by any one individual but by one overriding problem, namely the industrialisation of the American economy. Industrialisation had brought in its train a variety of social and economic problems. Individual state governments had tried to lessen the effects of industrialisation by passing laws that, for example, controlled the hours of work and wages of all women and children, as well as men who were in the more dangerous occupations. The problem for the Supreme Court was whether these pieces of legislation were constitutional. The principal constitutional barrier was, ironically, the Fourteenth Amendment to the Constitution which was passed after the Civil War to help the freed slaves. The Fourteenth Amendment contained a due process clause, which was used by those who opposed the social reforms to question the constitutionality of the legislation. Most students of the Supreme Court believe it was, in the post-Civil War period, sympathetic to the opponents of reform and to the interests of the propertied classes in general. Certainly on numerous occasions the Court did hold to be unconstitutional legislation which limited the number of hours that could be worked. A good example of such a case is *Lochner* v. *New York* (1905), when the Court held that a state law regulating the hours of bakery workers was unconstitutional. However, whether the Court was politically biased is more debatable (see below). Nevertheless, the decisions of the Court, once again, had great significance for American society.

The New Deal Court

One of the most dramatic conflicts between the presidency and the Supreme Court occurred in the 1930s. Franklin D. Roosevelt was elected to the presidency in 1932 at the depth of the Great Depression. During the campaign he had promised the American electorate a New Deal, which would combat the economic havoc of the depression. Owing to the economic crisis, the Congress passed Roosevelt's proposals with remarkable speed, even though they were complex, affected virtually every major aspect of American economic life, and vastly increased the role of the federal government in the economy. Unfortunately for Roosevelt and the New Deal, the Supreme Court did not accept that a great number of these laws were constitutional, and, starting in 1935, several major pieces of New Deal legislation were held unconstitutional. A good example of the Court's decisions is *United States* v. *Butler* (1936), which held the agricultural recovery programme invalid. Publicly, Roosevelt attacked the Court in reasonably moderate language. Privately, he was furious, and, when he was re-elected in 1936 by a landslide, he proposed to the Congress that the number of Supreme Court judges be increased from nine to fifteen. President Roosevelt claimed that he was suggesting the change because he was concerned for the efficiency of the Court. However, everyone else realised that this was a smokescreen and the episode became known as the 'Court-packing fight' because Roosevelt was attempting to pack the Court with his own appointees. There are three important points to note from the Court-packing episode:

(a) *Roosevelt lost*; his proposals were defeated in the Congress. Roosevelt was an immensely popular President who had just been re-elected by an overwhelming majority; nevertheless he suffered his first major defeat in the Congress. The Court's decisions on the New Deal were very unpopular indeed, but even so the Congress and the electorate were loath to tamper with the Supreme Court.

(b) *The Court appeared to change direction in 1937*. There is considerable disagreement over whether the Court deliberately reversed itself over the New Deal to undercut the Court-packing plans, but there certainly was a change in the Court's attitude. From mid-1937 onwards, the Court left the New Deal programmes alone.

(c) *The conflict over the New Deal illustrates the power of the Court, plus the regard and esteem with which it is held, even when its decisions are unpopular*. Perhaps this episode also illustrates the fact that the Court is aware that, in the final analysis, its power rests on consent and that its decisions cannot stray too far from what is acceptable to the electorate and the electorate's representatives.

The modern Supreme Court

The Warren Court (1954–69)
When President Dwight D. Eisenhower in 1954 nominated Earl Warren as Chief Justice, no one expected, least of all President Eisenhower, that the Supreme Court was about to embark on a period of quite remarkable activity. The Warren Court was, without a doubt, one of the great reforming courts of American judicial history. There are two characteristics which distinguish the Warren Court from its predecessors.

(*a*) *It was almost entirely unconcerned with economic issues*, unlike the New Deal Court or the post-Civil War Courts. The Warren Court was preoccupied with civil rights, i.e., the rights of black Americans, and civil liberties.

(*b*) *Whereas the Supreme Court had previously been interested in limiting the role of government, the Warren Court increased the obligations of government*. Many of the decisions of the Court, between 1954 and 1964, attempted to use government, both state and federal, as an instrument of reform. Clearly the justices on the Warren Court harboured more positive attitudes towards government than the predecessors.

The Warren Court and civil rights
The Warren Court will perhaps be best remembered for its decisions over civil rights. Certainly its most famous decision was *Brown* v. *Board of Education* (1954). Until the *Brown* case all Southern states used to segregate the races. Separate schools were provided for black and white children. There were seats specifically designated for blacks and whites on buses and trains. Hotels, swimming pools, public parks excluded one race or the other. In 1896 the Supreme Court, in *Plessy* v. *Ferguson*, said racial segregation was constitutionally acceptable. However, the Court in *Brown* v. *Board of Education* reversed the *Plessy* decision. The constitutional argu-

ment revolved around the Fourteenth Amendment, and more particularly its equal protection clause. In *Plessy* the Court had declared that the equal protection clause permitted 'separate but equal' treatment, i.e., the races could be segregated as long as the facilities provided for both races were equal. In 1954 the Warren Court, interpreting the same equal protection clause, said that racial separation was inherently unequal. Segregation, claimed Chief Justice Warren, the author of the opinion in *Brown*, psychologically damaged black children and therefore was unequal. Of course this decision had the most enormous impact on American society. Southern whites were furious and up in arms, but the most lasting impact of *Brown* was its stimulus on the civil rights movement and the role it played in bringing about further changes in the law a decade later with the Civil Rights Act of 1964.

The Warren Court and legislative apportionment   Until the 1960s there was no uniform rule which governed the size of legislative constituencies in the United States. The individual state legislatures drew up constituency boundaries, and the principles they used to do so varied enormously. The principle which was perhaps uniform to all state legislatures was that the majority party attempted to gain as much political benefit as possible by concentrating their opponents' strengths in a few constituencies while dispersing their own voters more widely. Consequently constituencies varied in shape and, most importantly, in population size. It was quite common twenty years ago to see a constituency which would have fourteen or fifteen times, and on occasion forty or fifty times, the population of another constituency. The political effect of the disparity in population was to over-represent rural areas and in some cases permit rural domination of state legislatures. In a series of decisions, of which the most important are *Baker* v. *Carr* (1962), *Wesberry* v. *Sanders* (1964) and *Reynolds* v. *Sims* (1964), the Warren Court insisted that legislative constituencies, for all state legislatures and for the House of Representatives, had to contain approximately the same population. The Court once again relied on the equal protection clause of the Fourteenth Amendment. On this issue, however, the Warren Court's interpretation of the equal protection clause was not unanimous. There were powerful dissenting voices on the Court, who believed that other justices of the court were going too far in imposing their own personal views on representation on the American people.

The Warren Court and the police   Another major area of reform for the Warren Court was in the area of the criminal suspect. The Court, or at least a majority of the justices on the Court, showed their suspicion that the police coerced confessions out of suspects. In *Miranda* v. *Arizona* (1966), interpreting the Fifth Amendment (protection against self-incrimination) to the Constitution, the Warren Court laid down very strict procedures which the police had to follow when questioning suspects. In other areas of the criminal law the Court interpreted the Sixth Amendment (right to legal counsel) to the Constitution in *Gideon* v. *Wainwright* (1963) to guarantee defendants a lawyer in all serious cases in state courts, even if the defendants could not afford a lawyer. The Court substantially tightened previous judicial interpretations of the Fourth Amendment (protection against unlawful search and seizure) to further restrict the discretion of the police.

The Warren Court – a summary   (*a*) *The Warren Court re-wrote the rules that governed:*

> (i) relations between blacks and whites in the South;
> (ii) relations between the police and the criminal suspect;
> (iii) the drawing of legislative constituencies.

It was a constitutional revolution.

(*b*) *The Warren Court's constitutional revolution, however, was not universally welcomed*. There were attempts to pass constitutional amendments to overturn some of these decisions. The Court and Earl Warren in particular, were not popular with American conservatives.

(*c*) *The Warren Court's record is once again a testament to the power of the Court*. The Warren Court's record also raises the question of whether the Supreme Court is too powerful. Why should the Warren Court have changed the balance between the police and the criminal suspect? Why did the Court impose a theory of representation – only population size counts – when the American Constitution itself organised the United States Senate on a territorial rather than population basis? Did the Warren

Court impose its own beliefs? Was the judiciary becoming to powerful?

The Burger Court (1969–86)

When President Richard M. Nixon nominated Warren E. Burger to succeed Earl Warren as Chief Justice, there was no doubt in Nixon's mind as to what he expected from Burger. A major element of Nixon's presidential campaign had been directed against the Warren Court and promised to appoint in their words 'strict constructionist' judges – i.e., judges who would interpret the Constitution and not impose their own beliefs – to the Supreme Court. Nixon was able to appoint three judges – Justices Blackmun, Powell and Rehnquist, in addition to Burger. Nixon's Republican successor Gerald Ford appointed a further judge, Mr Justice Stevens. In 1981 President Reagan appointed Sandra D. O'Connor. So how have the Nixon/Ford/Regan appointees fared? Did they succeed in imposing a judicial conservatism after the reforms of Warren? The simple answer is no. The Burger Court is difficult to label – much more so than the Warren Court. It is far more elusive to classify. A few examples will demonstrate the reasons for this statement.

The Burger Court and civil rights

After the *Brown* case had decided that racial segregation was unconstitutional, the problem that faced the judiciary was examining how best racial integration and racial equality could be achieved. Two devices were proposed to achieve these ends. The first was busing. The second was positive discrimination.

(*a*) *Busing*. Busing involves black and white children being transported in order to achieve a balance between the races in all the schools within the jurisidiction of a local authority. In *Swann* v. *Charlott-Mecklenburg Board of Education* (1971), the Burger Court endorsed the Constitutionality of busing.

(*b*) *Positive discrimination* or Affirmative Action policies essentially involve discriminating in favour of minority groups, particularly blacks. Positive discrimination programmes were developed in the 1970s to assist blacks in university admissions, training programmes and employment generally. The question that hung over these schemes was whether they were

constitutional. The Burger Court had indicated in cases like
Regents of the University of California v. *Bakke* (1978) that the
principle of positive discrimination is constitutional. However,
in a 1984 case, *Firefighters Local Union No. 1784* v. *Stotts* the
Court appeared to be somewhat less enthusiastic about affirmative action.

The Burger Court and civil liberties   The Burger Court has most
probably been a disappointment to its conservative sponsors in
the area of civil liberties. Admittedly the Burger Court has eroded
to some extent the limitations on the power of the police imposed
by the Warren Court. However, the other areas, the Burger Court
has protected traditional civil liberties and has also broken new
constitutional ground. In the Pentagon Papers Case, *The New
York Times Co.* v. *United States* (1971), the Court upheld the
freedom of the press, despite an attempt by the Nixon administration to prevent two leading newspapers from publishing
classified material on the Vietnam war. In *Roe* v. *Wade* (1973),
the Court broke new ground by declaring that a woman has a
constitutional entitlement to an abortion. Neither of these
decisions pleased the Nixon administration nor did the next case,
which has had, to date, the most immediate and significant
political impact.

United States* v. *Richard M. Nixon (1974)   This case arose out of
the Watergate scandal (see Chapter 5), where seven high-ranking
officials, close to President Nixon, were charged with a conspiracy to violate a variety of criminal laws. Nixon himself was under
suspicion and, unfortunately for him, evidence was available
which would prove or disprove his involvement in the conspiracy.
Nixon had installed in the White House a tape-recording system.
Therefore there were tapes available of all conversations to the
Oval Office. The officials investigated the Watergate affair
obtained a court order to compel Nixon to release the tapes.
Nixon refused on the grounds that the conversations were
privileged to the executive branch and no other branch of
government had an entitlement to hear the tapes. The Supreme
Court then had to decide between the competing claims. On the
one hand there was a claim for *executive privilege*, on the other
the claim of the investigating team was the need to obtain
evidence for a possible criminal prosecution. On 24 July 1974,

Chief Justice Burger, speaking for a unanimous Court, held the need for evidence in a criminal proceeding must be paramount and consequently Nixon's claim of executive privilege was dismissed. As a result of *United States* v. *Richard M. Nixon* the tapes were released and some two weeks later President Nixon resigned.

The Burger Court – a summary

(*a*) It is difficult to label the Burger Court. It is not as easy to categorise as the Warren Court.

(*b*) The hopes or fears that it would overturn the Warren Court's decisions have not come to pass.

(*c*) The Nixon-appointed justices did not show, either in the Pentagon Papers case or the Watergate tapes case, any partiality to the Nixon administration.

The Rehnquist Court

When Chief Justice Burger resigned in 1986, President Reagan appointed Associate Justice William Rehnquist to fill the vacancy. The object of the appointment was to continue the administration's attempt to encourage the Supreme Court in a more conservative direction. Rehnquist's place, in turn, was filled by Antonin Scalia, who also conformed to the criteria laid down by Reagan's Attorney-General, Edwin Meese. But perhaps the clearest indication of the administration's intentions occurred during the unsuccessful nomation of Robert Bork. Bork was a distinguished judge and had been an equally distinguished law professor; although throughout his career as judge and professor, he had never disguised his 'conservative preferences'. He also had been even more controversially, an important participant in the dismissal of the Special Watergate Prosecutor, Archibald Cox, that had occurred during the prolonged and painful death of the Nixon presidency. In short, Bork was a very controversial figure, but nevertheless he was nominated by President Reagan because both the President and Ed Meese believed that he and the other Reagan appointees would lead the Supreme Court in the direction that the administration wanted. However, the Senate refused to confirm the Bork nomination after one of the most intense and bitter confirmation battles.

The Reagan administration, having lost the battle for Bork, may not have lost the war. The President subsequently nominated

Charles Kennedy, who was confirmed relatively easily by the Senate even though Kennedy supported the same broad positions taken by Bork, although with greater diplomacy and discretion. Moreover, the election of George Bush has given the Republicans four more years in which to make further judicial appointments. It is more than probable that Bush will have the opportunity to nominate several justices. Justices Blackmun, Brennan and Marshall are over eighty and are likely to resign in the near future. If President Bush and his Attorney-General, Richard Thornburgh, take the same view of appointments as their predecessors, than the impact on the Court may well be substantial, while one must always remember that appointments do not invariably work out in the manner that Presidents intend. But returning to the president, in what way have the Reagan appointees begun to influence the direction of the Rehnquist Court?

It is too early to offer a definitive answer to this question. The early indications are that the Rehnquist Court will be far more cautious than either the Warren or Burger Courts. This caution suggests that there will not be any sudden shifts in direction or any radical new departure, which were features of the Warren and Burger years. The Court is very unlikely to stake out new territory that the Warren Court did so frequently and that the Burger Court did somewhat less frequently. Of course this caution will also mean that the Rehnquist Court is unlikely to overturn, at least directly, the most contentious decisions of recent years, on abortion and affirmative action. The Court is far more likely to chip away at these decisions and an indication of this was given in the affirmative action programme operated by the city of Richmond, Virginia. This case suggests that affirmative action programmes are going to be closely examined by the Court in the future. What is certain is that the Rehnquist Court will be very closely observed over the new few years to see whether the long promised judicial counter-revolution has finally arrived.

The appointment of Supreme Court justices

President Nixon's disappointment with the Burger Court was only the latest expression of presidential disillusionment with their judicial appointees. President Eisenhower is known to have regretted the appointment of Warren. President Harry S. Truman said that his appointment of Justice Tom C. Clark – 'that damn

THE SUPREME COURT AND THE JUDICIAL PROCESS

fool from Texas' – was his 'biggest mistake'. Why then are Presidents to frequently disappointed? The reasons perhaps lie in the appointment process. What then are the reasons behind presidential selection?

(*a*) *A judge is frequently chosen because he is a member of a particular racial or religious group*. President Lyndon Johnson, for example, nominated Thurgood Marshall in 1967. Marshall was chosen because he was black, in addition to being an able lawyer. At other times there has been a catholic or Jewish 'seat' on the Court. President Reagan's appointment of a woman, Sandra D. O'Connor, reflected the same motivation; a desire on the part of a president to improve his relations with a specific group.

(*b*) *Presidents trade the power of judicial appointment for other favours*. It is a well-established rumour that Eisenhower appointed Warren because Warren agreed to help Eisenhower in his bid for the 1952 Republican presidential nomination.

(*c*) *Presidents wish to change the direction of the Court's decisions*. The best recent example is, of course, Nixon, who wished to counteract the 'liberalism' of the Warren Court. He chose 'conservative' laywers as his appointees (two of whom, Clement Haynesworth and Harold Carswell, were not approved by the United States Senate).

(*d*) *The common factor in the above three reasons is the political advantage which the President believes he will gain from the appointment*. Even Nixon's apparent ideological reasons have a sound political rationale. He believed the Warren Court was deeply unpopular and his 'conservative' choices would gain him political approval. Perhaps this is the reason why Presidents are so often disappointed by the judicial appointments.

The Supreme Court – a judicial or political institution?

Presidents are fully aware of the enormous political impact of Supreme Court decisions. Unfortunately they tend to assume that because the judgements have political consequences, the decisions must have also been motivated by politics. Consequently, Presidents believe that if they appoint political allies or ideological bedfellows, they will have a pliant and congenial Supreme

Court. As we have seen, this has not been the case, because of one very important reason. *The Supreme Court is not only a political institution. It is also a judicial and legal body and its judicial and legal characteristics must not be underestimated.* For example, Warren was a moderately conservative Republican governor of California before becoming Chief Justice. According to Eisenhower and other politicians, Warren's judicial career was 'out of character'. In another sense, however, it was very in character. Warren conformed to the ethos and requirements of the Supreme Court. What then are these judicial and legal characteristics of the Supreme Court?

(*a*) *It is a court.* It can only decide those issues which are brought to it through litigation.

(*b*) *It is like any other court.* Technical legal factors play an important role and can determine particular decisions.

(*c*) *The legal process as a whole requires a measure of certainty.* Judges therefore have a restricted discretion. They are limited by previous decisions. Supreme Court judges are not bound by earlier rulings but they do have to weigh them very seriously indeed.

(*d*) *The ethos of the Court is non-political.* Supreme Court justices do not think of themselves as politicians. This self-image is important as it affects their behaviour.

(*e*) *Because they do not think of themselves as politicians*, they usually sever any partisan connection and distance themselves from everyday political activity.

(*f*) *Judges can and do distinguish between their personal preferences and what they believe the law requires.* There are many examples of judges who say, 'I would prefer this but the Constitution requires the reverse.'

Of course, this does not mean that the Supreme Court does not have a political role. It does. Because of judicial review it cannot avoid a political role. But that does not mean judges are politicians. It is the unique characteristic of the American political system that judges provide constitutional solutions to political problems.

Further reading

V. Blasi (ed.), *The Burger Court*, Yale University Press, 1983.

R. Hodder-Williams, *The Politics of the U.S. Supreme Court*, Allen & Unwin, 1980.

Richard Maidment, 'The Burger Court in retrospect', in D.   K. Adams (ed.), *Studies in American Politics*, Manchester University Press, 1989.

5

PRESIDENTIAL POWER

Shortly before President Harry S. Truman (1945–53) was to leave office, he was asked how he thought his successor, Dwight D. Eisenhower (1953–61) would cope with being President of the United States. 'He'll sit here,' said Truman, pointing to his desk, 'and he'll say, "Do this! Do that!" And nothing will happen. Poor Ike . . . He will find it very frustrating.' This forecast of presidential impotence appeared to contradict a slogan that Truman used to keep on his desk in the Oval Office of the White House, 'The buck stops here.' What did the slogan mean? It meant that while other individuals or bodies within the executive branch or in the other branches of government could avoid and pass on the responsibility for making decisions, the President could not do so. He could not avoid the responsibility of decision-making and hand it over to another institution or another person. Truman personally had made the very difficult decision to drop the A-bomb on Japan in 1945, and he also ordered American troops to South Korea in 1950. The buck had stopped, for Truman, in the Oval Office of the White House. So do Truman's remarks about Eisenhower, or the slogan on his desk, provide the more accurate judgement on the presidency? The argument still continues. Within the past decade the presidency of Richard Nixon (1969–74) was seen by many political commentators as being too dangerously powerful for the health of the American political system. Within a few years of Nixon's resignation, however, the worries that the presidency was too powerful had evaporated and in fact the principal worry about the institution was exactly the reverse. Jimmy Carter (1977–81) was frequently criticised for being too weak and for not providing adequate leadership. 'More mush from the wimp', was how a major American newspaper contemptuously described an important speech by President Carter. So is the American presidency too weak or too powerful? This chapter will try to deal with this key question among others.

The presidency and the Constitution

As we have seen in Chapter 1, the framers of the Constitution in 1787 were unsure about the institution of the presidency for reasons very similar to those mentioned above. They wanted an executive branch which had an independent base of authority and which could resist any improper actions, particularly by the legislative branch, but at the same time they were worried about the presidency having too much power. The Convention wanted a national leader but feared the creation of a tyrant. Inevitably, the institution that emerged reflected these hopes and fears.

The powers of the President

(a) The President is the head of the executive branch (Article II Section I).

(b) The President is the commander-in-chief of the armed forces (Article II Section II).

(c) The President has the power to make treaties (Article II Section II).

(d) The President has the authority to appoint ambassadors, Cabinet officers, Supreme Court judges, etc. (Article II Section II).

(e) The President can veto a bill which has been passed by both houses of Congress (Article I Section VII).

(f) The President is entitled to make recommendations on legislation to the Congress (Article II Section III).

Limitations on the powers of the President

(a) The President can be removed from office through the process of being impeached (charged) and then being found guilty of treason, bribery or other high crimes and misdemeanours.

(b) Although the President is the commander-in-chief of the armed forces, the Congress retains the right to declare war and to raise the money to pay for the armed forces (Article I Section VIII).

(*c*) Although the President has the power to make treaties, such treaties must be approved by a two-thirds majority of the Senate (Article II Section II).

(*d*) Similarly, the President's power of appointment is subject to Senate approval (Article II Section II).

(*e*) The President's veto of a bill passed by Congress can be overturned by a two-thirds majority in each house of Congress.

The Constitution thus reflect the ambivalence that the members of the Constitutional Convention felt towards the presidency. The President had to be given specific powers, independent of the legislative branch, but he had to be controlled. The Convention was perhaps more sure of the role they expected the presidency to play in the American system of government. As the presidency was more insulated from the electorate (see Chapter 1) than either of the houses of Congress, it was likely that the presidency would be a more responsible institution restraining the more radical impulses of Congress, particularly the House of Representatives. The House of Representatives would provide new ideas, energy and the impetus for change; the presidency would contribute a restraining hand.

The growth of presidential power 1789–1933

George Washington and the office of presidency
It was clear from the very first president, George Washington (1789–97), that the office of the presidency was going to play a somewhat different role than that intended in the Constitution. The President was capable of initiating actions and doing so quickly. President Washington acted decisively, particularly in the field of foreign affairs. For example, American neutrality in the war between the French and the British was established by a presidential initiative. He not only created the presidential Cabinet system, but it was said that he was the master of every detail of administration. Washington's greatest contribution to the presidency was that by the time he left office in 1797, the presidency was established. Through his political skill the presidency was endowed with dignity, authority ad legitimacy.

The increase in presidential initiative
Some of Washington's successors were also capable of significant

presidential initiatives. Thomas Jefferson (1801–09) committed the United States to the purchase of the vast territory of French Louisiana from France in 1803 without consulting the Congress. Andrew Jackson (1829–37) asserted the power and the authority of the presidency at the expense of Congress. Jackson's assertion of presidential power was an interesting reversal of constitution intentions for Jackson was known as the 'People's President', and the presidency was the democratic radical insititution fighting against a conservative legislature. Perhaps the most dramatic exercise of presidential power in the nineteenth century was during the American Civil War. Because of this crisis, Abraham Lincoln (1861–65) simply assumed that the President could authorise certain actions without the prior approval of the Congress. For example, he imposed a blockade on the Southern states which had decided to leave the Union. He enlarged the size of the army and navy beyond the legal limits. Lincoln's presidency established precedents for presidential actions. The authority and power of the presidency was substantially increased, and the Congress accepted this presidential domination. Similarly during the First World War, Woodrow Wilson (1913–21) made the presidency the central instrument in the organisation and leadership of America's war effort. So from 1789 until 1933 there are many examples of presidential leadership, and the dramatic exercise of presidential power, and undoubtedly the presidency came to play a more central role than was intended in the American political system. However, the power of the presidency in this period can be exaggerated.

Congress and the presidency
Many of the periods of presidential power were followed by periods of congressional resurgence. The presidencies of Jefferson, Jackson and particularly of Lincoln and Wilson were succeeded by a Congress anxious to reassert itself. Thus the authority of the presidency between 1789 and 1933 tended to vary with the personality of the President and the nature of events. Presidential power tended to ebb and flow. Lincoln was followed by Andrew Johnson (1865–69) and Ulysses S. Grant (1869–77), and Wilson by Warren G. Harding (1921–23) and Calvin Coolidge (1923–29), none of whom were deemed to be successful because their lives were made difficult by a Congress anxious to cut the presidency down to size. Andrew Johnson's life was

particularly difficult as he bears the unwelcome distinction of being the only President to have been impeached, although he was not found guilty. So by 1933, although the presidency was playing a larger role than constitutionally intended, nevertheless the fundamental relationship particularly between itself and the Congress would have been recognisable to the members of the 1787 Convention. However, the constitutional balance was about to be dramatically changed.

The modern presidency (from 1933)

The shape of the presidency was fundamentally altered after 1933 by two developments:

(a) *The involvement of the federal government in the nation's economic life.* This process essentially started with the New Deal reforms in the first administration of Franklin D. Roosevelt (1933–45).

(b) *The end of American isolationism in 1941 when America entered the Second World War.* After the Second World War the United States did not retreat into isolationism, as it had done after the First World War, but played a full role in the international community.

Both of these developments have had the consequence of increasing the importance of the executive branch at the expense of the legislative branch.

The United States has been no different from other Western societies in seeing a substantial growth in the size of bureaucracies to cope with the increasing responsibility of central government to deal with the nation's economic and social problems. The federal government's departments and agencies have grown enormously both in number and size (see Chapter 9). But just as important as the growth of the federal bureaucracy has been the Congress's willingness to accept that it is the responsibility of the executive branch to administer these new programmes, to devise new ones and to suggest a list of priorities as to which new proposals and policies should be enacted into law. Since 1933 it has become expected of the President to present a comprehensive legislative programme to the Congress for consideration. This was not the case before 1933, but it is now a routine procedure.

American involvement in the world community has also increased the importance of the presidency in the American system of government, because foreign relations have always been seen as an area particularly suited to presidential action. Diplomacy often requires secrecy and speed, particularly in the nuclear age, and the Congress cannot provide either. Hence, the President has always been pre-eminent in foreign affairs. While the United States cut itself off from the rest of the world, this did not affect the constitutional balance between President and Congress. However, from 1941 onwards when the United States entered the Second World War, America's relations with the rest of the world could be said to be of greater importance than many domestic issues. American Presidents have automatically become world figures, and their skill in diplomacy and their conduct of foreign affairs have often been vital to the success of their term in office. So, as foreign relations have absorbed the interest of the American electorate, from the Second World War through the Cold War and its crises to the present day, the presidency, not the Congress, has been the central focus for their concerns.

These two developments have greatly increased the responsibilities of the presidency since 1933. Inevitably, there arise two questions: how has the presidency coped with these responsibilities, and what have been the consequences of this enlarged role for the American political system? Before these questions can be dealt with satisfactorily, we must examine the institutions and procedures which have developed over the past half-century to assist the presidency in the fulfilment of these new responsibilities and duties.

The growth of the federal bureaucracy

As mentioned above, there has been an enormous increase in the number of federal civil servants over the past five decades, and without this increase the presidency would not be able to cope with the current demands and requirements. The federal bureaucracy is the instrument for transmitting information to and from the presidency, organising and devising legislative proposals and implementing legislation. However, the bureaucracy's growth has been a mixed blessing to the presidency. The President is constitutionally the head of the executive branch of government. The civil service exists to assist the President in the exercise of his duties. The civil servants should execute the orders and instructions of the President. However, various Presidents, along with politicians in other Western countries, have discovered that political reality often differs from the formal legal position. The federal civil service can often be as much a hindrance to the President as it can be of help. Franklin Roosevelt once described the process of bringing about change in the Navy Department: '[it's similar] to punching a feather bed. You punch it with your right and you punch it with your left until you are finally exhausted, and then you find the damn bed just as it was when you started punching.' In recent years Presidents have felt even more antagonistic about the departments. Richard Nixon, a conservative Republican, believed that the bureaucracy was composed of liberal Democrats who wished to sabotage his policies. In particular he had grave suspicions about the State Department (the department in charge of foreign affairs). The interesting thing about Nixon's suspicions is that all Presidents in recent times, regardless of party, have not trusted their civil servants and have been wary of their advice. Presidents, however, have alternative sources of advice and information: they can turn to their own staff.

The presidential staff

The growth of the presidential advisory staff has been perhaps the most significant development in the presidency in recent years. The importance of the presidential staff stems from the fact that they are appointed by the President and remain in office only as long as he does, and less if he chooses to remove them. They have no security of appointment – their position is dependent on the President. As a result the President trusts his staff politically and prefers their advice to that which he gets from the various civil service departments. The size of the presidential staff has grown enormously in recent years, from 1,098 in 1940 to 5,722 in 1972. By 1980, because of Watergate, the official numbers had been reduced to 1,735, but this figure substantially underestimated the actual number of presidential staff. Consequently the range of advice and expertise has grown, and almost permits a President to depend entirely on his own staff and ignore the federal bureaucrats. Most members of the presidential staff are organised within the Executive Office of the President.

The Executive Office of the President

In 1937 the President's Committee on Administrative Management, known as the Brownlow Committee, examined the administration of the federal government and declared, 'The President needs help'. Two years later the Executive Office of the President was created. This is composed of a number of organisations, some of which were already in existence in 1939, such as the Office of Management and Budget (OMB), and others which have been added subsequently, such as the Office of Civil and Defense Mobilization (OCDM) in 1958. The principal components of the Executive Office are:

(a) *The National Security Council (NSC).* The NSC was established in 1947 to advise the President on 'domestic, foreign and military policies relating to the national security'. The NSC is often a more influential body than the State Department on foreign policy matters. Between 1969 and 1973, during the first term of Richard Nixon's presidency, the most senior staff member of the NSC, the Assistant to the President for National Security Affairs, was Henry Kissinger. Clearly Nixon preferred the advice of Kissinger and the NSC to the advice of the State Department and his Secretary of State, William Rogers. Similarly President Carter relied heavily on Zbigniew Brzezinski and the NSC. President Reagan's Assistant to the President for National Security Affairs was William Clark, but it is less certain that Reagan has followed Nixon and Carter and prefers the NSC to the State Department.

(b) *Council of Economic Advisers (CEA).* The CEA was established in 1946 to advise the President on economic matters, offering the President an alternative source of advice to the Treasury Department. Once again in recent years Presidents have preferred their own CEA to the bureaucrats of the Treasury.

(c) *The Office of Policy Development (OPD).* This was established in 1981 by President Reagan to offer him advice on domestic policy over a wide range of issues. The intention behind the creation of the OPD was yet again to provide the President with alternative advice, this time in the field of domestic policy.

(d) *White House Office.* The White House Office incorporates those functions which require the closest daily contact with the President. Inevitably these positions are filled by those who are closest politically to the President, normally by those who have worked in the presidential campaign. They are often known as Special Assistants to the President and their specific duties vary from President to President. The size of the White House Office has grown substantially from 63 in 1940 to 351 in 1980.

(e) *The Office of Management and Budget (OMB)*. The OMB was already in existence in 1939, although it was then known as the Bureau of the Budget. The OMB is a vital element of the Executive Office as it assists the President in the preparation of his budget and in the planning of his legislative proposals to the Congress.

The budget and the President's legislative programme
Each year the President prepares a budget and a legislative programme, both of them important instruments of presidential power. Every year the various departments of the federal government inform the OMB both of their financial requirements and suggestions for legislation, which they hope will be included in the programme of legislation that the President will present to Congress. The OMB assesses these submissions, frequently modifying them, and uses them to construct the budget and legislative programme. The importance of this procedure is that annual review by the OMB is the only one of its kind. The OMB has to evaluate the total range of activities of the federal government and therefore is able to develop an overall picture of the needs and requirements of the federal government. Because it is the only picture available and is developed within the presidency, it gives the President a substantial advantage in his relations with the Congress and the federal bureaucracy. This advantage was considered to be so substantial that new congressional Budget Committees were formed in the mid-1970s, in order to lessen the dependence of the Congress on the President's budget. It is not easy to measure the success of the new Budget Committees.

Congressional acceptance of presidential leadership
This has been particularly true in the field of foreign affairs. Ever since the onset of the Cold War in 1947 the Congress has been willing to give the President considerable freedom in foreign and defence matters. Between 1947 and 1970 the Congress only very

rarely questioned presidential initiatives in foreign policy, and then usually urged the President to be firm in his dealings with the Soviet Union. However, the problems caused by the Vietman War did bring about a period of congressional challenge to presidential leadership in foreign affairs, most notably with the passage of the War Powers Act of 1973, which placed congressional limitations on the power of the President to send troops abroad. More recently the Senate refused to ratify the Second Strategic Arms Limitation Treaty (SALT II). However, there were indications that the Congress in the first term of the Reagan presidency is now more willing to accept a greater degree of presidential leadership, as seen in its acceptance of President Reagan's proposed reductions in government expenditure.

The President's Cabinet

The Cabinet is not usually viewed as an instrument of presidential power. It is made up of heads of the major civil service departments plus anyone else whom the President chooses to invite. Although members of the Cabinet may be powerful and important individually, collectively the Cabinet is not an important institution. Members of the Cabinet prefer to discuss issues directly and privately with the President rather than in the cabinet room. Nevertheless, most recent Presidents, including Ronald Reagan, have claimed that they wished to see the Cabinet become an important decision-making body. However, usually within a year or two of the start of their administration, Presidents have found the Cabinet as a collective unit less than useful, and have relied increasingly on private discussions with individual members of the Cabinet and on the presidential staff. Perhaps the famous remark of Abraham Lincoln's illustrates the lack of regard that most Presidents come to have of their Cabinets. After a vote in a Cabinet meeting when the President voted yes, Lincoln is claimed to have said 'seven noes, one aye – and ayes have it'.

The imperial presidency?

By the early 1970s political commentators, for the reasons mentioned above, began to believe that the presidency had become too powerful. Arthur Schlesinger Jr, the distinguished historian, coined the phrase 'The Imperial Presidency'. He and others suggested that the constitutional balance between the

institutions of the federal government had tilted dangerously in
favour of the presidency. They pointed to the growth of the
Executive Office of the President and presidential domination of
foreign policy in particular. The presidency, in the view of these
observers, was carrying out the duties and tasks which were
reserved for the Congress or at least shared between the branches.
This analysis was widely accepted because, as we have seen, the
presidency was a more powerful institution than fifty years
previously, but also because the United States had suffered two
major crises, Vietnam and Watergate, which appeared to be
explainable by the notion of an 'Imperial Presidency'.

The Vietnam episode

The United States involvement in the affairs of South Vietnam
was gradual and can be traced back to the years just after the end
of the Second World War. The introduction of large numbers of
American troops to South Vietnam, however, occurred only in
1965. By 1968 there were approximately half a million American
troops attempting to ensure that South Vietnam maintained a
non-communist government. Several political commentators,
including Arthur Schlesinger Jr, believe that the American
military involvement was due principally to the presidency, and
the President they primarily blame is Lyndon B. Johnson (1963–
69). They argue that Johnson misled the Congress and took the
United States down the path of military involvement by stealth,
and that, once American troops were stationed in South Vietnam,
the hands of the Congress were tied. These historians and political
scientists point to the legal basis of the American involvement in
South Vietnam, the Gulf of Tonkin Resolution, as symptomatic
of presidential deception. The Gulf of Tonkin Resolution was
passed almost unanimously by the Congress in 1964 in order to
allow the President to authorise whatever action was necessary to
deal with the unprovoked aggression from communist North
Vietnam. However, argue Schlesinger and others, the Congress
might not have passed the Resolution had it known that the
United States was conducting secret military operations against
the North. Furthermore, the Resolution was proposed by
Johnson as a response to a specific unprovoked North Vietnamese attack on American naval vessels in international waters.
However, in retrospect it can be seen that the attack may well
have been in retaliation to an earlier American operation and

could well have taken place in North Vietnamese waters. Further, it is now known that Johnson did not draft the resolution after this specific episode with the North Vietnamese, but had been carrying a copy of the resolution with him for several months awaiting a suitable opportunity to make it public. Consequently, Schlesinger and the others believe that Johnson led the Congress and the nation into war without any major congressional debate, let alone a congressional declaration of war.

Watergate

The Watergate affair took place during the presidency of Richard Nixon. During the 1972 presidential election campaign the Washington DC headquarters of the Democratic Party, based in the Watergate building, were burgled. The burglary was organised by employees of the campaign organisation supporting President Nixon, the Committee to Re-elect the President (CREEP). After the burglary, President Nixon and several close advisers on the presidential staff attempted to obstruct the process of justice, by misleading the criminal investigation into the burglary. Specifically they attempted to show that there were no connections between the burglars and members of the White House staff and in doing so tried to subvert the investigation by improper influence. Furthermore, apart from the burglary and the cover-up, other abuses of power by the Nixon administration emerged. The President and some of his close aides attempted to use certain highly sensitive government agencies, specifically the Central Intelligence Agency (CIA), the Federal Bureau of Investigation (FBI) and the Internal Revenue Service (IRS) for their own private political benefit. There were also several allegations of bribery, and successful attempts by private interests to buy influence and affect decisions within the Nixon administration. Inevitably, Watergate and the other associated horrors raised the problem of excessive presidential power and control of the President. But is the fear of an over-powerful presidency justified?

There is another side to the argument that the presidency is too powerful:

> (*a*) *During the Vietnam episode the Congress chose to accept President Johnson's leadership.* Indeed one could go further and say that Congress was even more aggressive than the presidency over the conduct of the war in Vietnam. There

was no significant opposition in Congress to the President's Vietnam policy in 1964/5 because Congress agreed with it. So the presidency did not deceive the Congress into the military intervention in South Vietnam, the Congress willingly went along with it. However, when support for Johnson's Vietnam policy in the country declined, so did it also in the Congress, and opposition was voiced.

(*b*) *Watergate did show that a President can abuse his power and authority, but it also demonstrated that the Congress can, if it desires, control the presidency.* If Richard Nixon had not resigned in August 1974, the House of Representatives would have impeached him. Indeed Nixon resigned because impeachment was a near-certainty.

(*c*) *If Congress can find the political determination to control the presidency, it will be able to do so.* After Watergate and Vietnam, the Congress did become more assertive. It passed the War Powers Act in 1973, mentioned above, and changed its budgetary procedures in an attempt to improve its position. This emergence of congressional determination can be attested to by Nixon's two immediate successors, Gerald Ford (1974–77) and Jimmy Carter (1977–81).

Presidential impotence?

By the end of Carter's presidency, the fears of an imperial presidency had receded. Instead they were replaced by the new worry that the presidency was impotent. Presidents Ford and Carter had been rebuffed by the Congress on several occasions. Important legislative proposals had been rejected by the Congress. Legislation on energy, the economy and SALT II did not find the Congress in a receptive mood. Consequently the presidency, in these seven years, appeared to provide very little leadership in domestic and foreign policy.

Once again these fears were somewhat exaggerated. Carter was not an inspirational figure, but his leadership deficiencies stemmed less from his own personal inadequacy, or the weakness of the office of president, than from the fact that the United States was unsure and divided over how to deal with its principal problems. For example, most Americans realised that energy consumption was too high; they were aware that oil consumption had to be reduced, but they were unwilling to accept the obvious solution, which was to increase the price of oil. Similarly in foreign affairs, Americans were unhappy with what they considered to be the expansionist foreign policy of the Soviet Union; they wished to resist it, but after Vietnam were wary of high military expenditure and foreign military commitments. This uncertainty was reflected in the Congress, and this was the problem that faced Ford and Carter and made it impossible for them to exercise leadership.

The Reagan years

When George Bush took the oath of office on 20 January 1989, his predecessor, Ronald Reagan, standing alongside the new President, could look back on eight years in the White House. This in itself was an achievement, for Reagan was the first American President in over a quarter of a century to have completed two terms in office. Moreover, his time in office is widely seen as having been successful. Certainly the American electorate's affection for Reagan has, if anything, grown over his term in office. His personal popularity, as he left Washington to return to California, was remarkably high; higher than that of any other President, at least since opinion polling began, at the end of their term of office. Most commentators have also given the Reagan administration relatively high marks, but is this approval deserved? Has the praise and affection been misplaced? So what have been the successes of the Reagan years and where has the Reagan administration been less than successful?

The restoration of American morale

Perhaps this has been the major achievement of the Reagan administration. The Vietnam and Watergate episodes severely eroded American confidence. The Ford and Carter presidencies did not restore the nation's morale and in certain respects they further worsened the problem. The growth of inflation, the inability to secure the return of the Iranian hostages, had increased the level of demoralisation. The United States in 1981 was unsure and uncertain of its role in the world. There was a lack of belief that the United States had the capacity and ability to control its future. The contrast with 1989 could not be more striking. The country's mood, as the Reagan years came to an end, was ebullient and confident. There has been a resurgence of patriotism and a restoration of national confidence, which in no small part has been due to personality of the President. He banished the introspection and self-doubt of the Jimmy Carter years and replaced them with a sunny self-assurance that most Americans found infectious.

The reduction in East/West tensions
It is an irony that the greatest achievement of the Reagan administration may well be that it was responsible for starting the process of ending the Cold War. It is an irony because Reagan had campaigned throughout his entire political career as a Cold Warrior. He was profoundly suspicious of the Soviet Union and characterised it as an 'Evil Empire'. He proposed to the Congress and obtained very substantial increases in defence spending. His first term as President was driven by a determination to be unyielding towards the Soviet Union. Nevertheless, during his second term, Reagan established a close working relationship with Mikhail Gorbachev and together they successfully negotiated a treaty that for the first time in post-war history would end the deployment of a specific category of nuclear weapons. It was a significant and historic achievement.

The growth of the economy
The restoration of American confidence was in part due to the longest period of unbroken growth in the economy since the end of the Second World War. The economic recession of the early 1980s was replaced by six years of consecutive economic growth, which also saw the rate of inflation fall while production, employment and incomes rose to unprecedented levels. There can be little doubt that the popularity of the administration of the President was greatly enhanced by the increased prosperity of most Americans.

The budget deficit
The prosperity of the Reagan years, however, was a consequence of economic policies that also led to very substantial deficits in the federal budget and in the nation's overseas trade. The Reagan strategy of lowering taxes and increasing defence expenditures without reducing other categories of federal spending proportionately, led to a cumulative budget deficit over the eight years of almost $1.5 trillion. In fiscal 1989 alone the federal deficit was

$160 billion and this was after several years of attempting to reduce the deficit! The consequences of this deficit have already been substantial. The increase in the national debt during the Reagan years has been greater than under all his predecessors combined. But more importantly, the deficit has been funded primarily by foreigners, particularly by Japanese financial institutions. The result has been to turn the United States from the world's leading creditor nation in 1981 to the world's largest debtor in 1989.

The trade deficit

The budget deficit has played its role in enlarging the balance of trade deficit by stimulating demand in the US economy to the extent that it could only be satisfied by foreign goods and services. In both 1986 and 1987 the trade deficit was running at approximately $140 billion per year. Most economists believe that this level of imbalance cannot be maintained without severe repercussions both for the United States as well as for the stability of the international economy.

The Reagan style

The Reagan years were a marked contrast to those of the Carter administration and nowhere was this contrast more marked than in the operating style of the Presidents. Carter was a 'hands on' President, anxious to be in command of all policy areas but perhaps overly interested and absorbed by detail. There is a story, possibly apocryphal, that Carter used to monitor the use of the tennis courts in the White House. Even if the story is not entirely accurate, it does illustrate the anxiety of President Carter to control all that occurred within the White House.

The operating style of the Reagan White House could not have been more different. The President was detached, to a quite striking degree, from the process of policy making. The numerous 'kiss and tell' memoirs of Reagan White House aides are in agreement that the President gave a very broad and general indication of where he wished to see policy changes, but after having done so did not involve himself in the detail of policy making. His Secretary of the Treasury during the first Reagan term, Donald Regan, did not speak to the President alone on matters of economic policy in four years. The advantages of the Reagan style was that the President's relative aloofness from policy-making process protected him from being overwhelmed by the day-to-day activities of politics. He was able to step back, retain his sense of perspective and his priorities and thereby give the nation an overall sense of direction. It also did permit his aides and Cabinet officers to get on with their jobs without constantly looking over their shoulders at the Oval Office. The disadvantages were that the President could be and was embarrassingly ill informed, on too many occasions, about matters of considerable national and international importance. No predecessor of recent memory has 'mis-spoken', to quote the White House, quite so frequently. But an even greater disadvantage was that the President's 'hands off' style allowed certain aides and officials a freedom that they abused. The one major scandal and indeed crisis of the Reagan administration, the Iran–Contra affair, arose out of this style of operation. Two officials within the National Security Council, John Poindexter, the National Security Adviser, and Oliver North, a relatively junior official, pursued a policy of selling arms to Iran in return for American hostages held in the Middle East. They then channelled the proceeds of the sale to the Contras, who were seeking to overthrow the left-wing government of Nicaragua. Both of these activities were illegal and only were able to take place because of the very permissive and lax procedures that President Reagan permited within his administration.

The Bush presidency (1989–   )

George Bush has become President at a time when relations between the United States and the Soviet Union have never been better since the two nations were allies during the Second World War. This provides the Bush administration with an opportunity to build on his predecessor's legacy and continue the process of lessening the tensions between the superpowers. The prospect is that the Bush administration will grasp this opportunity, although cautiously and carefully. Bush is less committed to the Strategic Defense Initiative – Star Wars – than was President Reagan, which may allow a greater degree of flexibility in US–Soviet negotiations.

The economic front poses greater problems for President Bush. The budget deficit appears to be especially intractable. The most memorable phrase of the 1988 presidential campaign was made by George Bush and then repeated virtually every day until the election: 'Read my lips, no new taxes.' If there are to be no new taxes, will there be reductions in federal expenditures? During the campaign, Bush made it clear that he did not favour any reductions in the defence budget, and the Congress, where control by the Democrats was strengthened by the 1988 elections, will not reduce non-defence expenditures. The result is likely to be an impasse, which will be both economically and politically difficult for the Bush administration to negotiate. It will be a major test for the political skill of the Bush administration.

Further reading

G. Hodgson, *All Things to All Men*, Penguin, 1984.

T. J. Lowi, *The Personal President: Power Invested, Promise Unfulfilled*, Cornell University Press, 1985.

R. Neustadt, *Presidential Power*, John Wiley, 1986.

Donald T. Regan, *For The Record*, Arrow, 1988.

Questions

1. To what extent did President Reagan restore the power and prestige to the office of the presidency?

2. Assess the importance of the the Executive Office of the President.

6

THE MODERN CONGRESS

Introduction

A recurrent theme in the early 1970s was that the role of Congress was being eroded and weakened in the face of what seemed to numerous commentators to be the inexorable expansion of presidential power. Yet simultaneously to students of legislative behaviour, the US Congress was perceived by many to be the most powerful national legislature in the Western democracies. These seemingly opposite views are perhaps best reconciled by Theodore Sorensen's comment that 'Congress already has enormous power, if only it had the guts to use it.'

Given that virtually everything the federal government does is reviewed, at least in part, by Congress, the legislature has immense scope for influencing public policy, yet for the most of its recent history has been dominated by the executive branch. In the last two decades Congressmen have attempted to redress this imbalance and reassert legislative power in the political system. How successful their attempts have been will now be assessed.

Congress and the Constitution

The Constitution made Congress the first branch of government. This reflected the political experiences of the Founding Fathers who regarded lawmaking as the major function of government, but who also regarded executive power with great distrust after their experiences with George III. Most of the powers and functions of Congress are set out in Article I, which defines its bicameral character and describes the internal operating procedures of the House of Representatives and the Senate. The Constitution, through the separation of powers, gives Congress an electoral and political independence from the executive branch of government, unlike the House of Commons, and it is this separation which provides the foundation for congressional authority.

Electoral independence

As noted in Chapter 1, members of Congress are elected independently from the President, the Constitution designating different constituencies and terms of office for the House and Senate.

1. House of Representatives This has 435 members, elected every two years, by the people from single-member districts apportioned to each state on a population basis, each state to have a minimum of one representative. Reapportionment occurs after each decennial census. In 1980, following re-districting, Florida, for example, gained 4 seats while New York lost 5. The redistribution of seats from the North-Eastern industrial states (the rustbelt) to the South and South-West (the sunbelt) reflects the nation's changing population base and thus changing political and economic centre of gravity.

2. The Senate This has 100 members, two for each state, elected for a six-year term, with one-third retiring every two years, Senators were originally elected by state legislatures, but since the enactment of the Seventeenth Amendment, are now chosen by popular vote.

The electoral independence that the Congress enjoys from the executive branch politically strengthens its Constitutional powers. In recent years different parties have been in control of the Congress and the White House. For example, 1968–76 Presidents Nixon and Ford (Republicans) held executive office while the Democrats were the majority party in Congress. From 1980 to 1986 Republican Ronald Reagan was president and the Grand Old Party (GOP) were the majority party in the Senate, but Democrats had a majority in the House of Representatives. By creating different electoral constituencies and terms of office between the President and Congress *and* between the House and

Senate the Founding Fathers sought to create political tensions and antagonisms between them.

Constitutional independence

Congress is granted specific authority in Article I. These powers can be divided into two broad categories.

(*a*) *Enumerated powers*. Section 8 lists seventeen specific powers. These include the power to declare war, to regulate interstate commerce and to coin money. The principle of enumerated powers means that Congress can only exercise those powers which are granted to it in the Constitution.

(*b*) *Implied powers*. The final clause in Section 8, known as the 'necessary and proper' clause, gives Congress the means to exercise enumerate powers. For example, the power to regulate interstate commerce (Clause 2) was joined to the 'necessary and proper' clause, to create the Interstate Commerce Commission which regulates economic activity between the states. Implied powers, by definition, expand on the enumerated powers grated to Congress by the Constitution.

The Constitution gives specific grants of authority to Congress as a whole, but each chamber also has special areas of responsibility.

(*a*) *The Senate* is allocated functions related closely to the executive branch. It has to 'advise and consent' to treaties, and to presidential appointments including ambassadors, Supreme Court justices and Cabinet members. Hence the Senate can influence appointments and the making of treaties. These constitutional responsibilities also are reflected in the prestige with which certain committee appointments are held. A seat on the Foreign Relations, Defense and Judiciary Committees is much sought after.

(*b*) *House of Representatives*. Today the major constitutional power left to the House is that of impeachment – the power to fomally charge the president and 'other civil officers' with 'Treason, Bribery or other High Crimes and Misdemeanors'. (The Senate acts as a Court to try impeachments.) Constitutionally all bills for raising revenue should originate in the House, but today the Senate plays a co-equal role. But the traditional pre-eminence of the House on finance matters led appointments to the Ways and Means, and Appropriations Committees being coveted.

Bi-cameral co-equality

On most legislative matters the House and Senate are co-equal partners. The 'power of the purse' means that no money can be spent by the executive unless it has been provided by Congress which gives it control over budgetary matters. Bills can be introduced in either chamber and, as they have to be approved by both houses, the legislature can often set the nation's policy agenda. As a bill on the same subject has to be passed in an identical version in both chambers (which is unlikely) there is pressure on members to work together to achieve compromise and co-operation in an institution where there is a tendency for political fragmentation.

Despite the pressures for co-operation between the House and Senate, there is also much rivalry, as they are different institutions in terms of membership, procedures and attitudes to public policy. This is not unexpected, given different constituency size: the average House district is 500,000 people while a Senate seat can be the size of California with a population of 10 million. The Senate is smaller, and has more staff, office space, committee appointments and more prestige than the House. The six-year electoral term, too, is said to insulate Senators from public opinion. However, since the defeat of certain prominent liberal senators in 1980, more attention has been paid to opinion back home by members of the upper chamber. On the other hand, House members, with a two-year term, pay assiduous attention to their districts, often visiting every weekend. Neither the House nor the Senate is more powerful than the other, but different constituencies, terms of office and constitutional responsibilities can create political tensions between both chambers, which make co-operation between the two sometimes difficult.

The rise and fall of congressional government

The constitutional factors outlined above, and in particular the powers granted in Congress in Article I Section 8, have structured the development and change which has occurred in the House and Senate. The framers of the Constitution intended Congress to have more authority than the President, and the legislative branch of government did indeed *make* laws. It is also significant that political parties first emerged in Congress. Congressional dominance, with only brief periods of executive importance, was maintained throughout the nineteenth century, and the constitutional authority was affirmed and expanded by Supreme Court decisions.

Congressional government

This is the title of a classic study by Woodrow Wilson, who in 1885 expressed concern at the development of congressional dominance, and in 1913 when he became President sought to increase executive power. Yet the constitutional autonomy of the House and Senate permits them to conduct business, consider bills or obtain information in ways determined by the members, and with funds appropriated to themselves from the Treasury. This is a strong advantage for the legislature, since it means that the executive cannot assume that its legislative initiatives will be accepted by the House and Senate. Only on very particular occasions is the President able to address the Congress in person, the separation of powers being a potent reality in practice. Liaison between the President and Congress therefore has to be created if the executive's legislative proposals are to be accepted. At times, albeit few and far between (the New Deal period of 1933–35, 1965–67 and 1981–82 being the most recent), Congress will accept executive proposals speedily in a range or policy areas. However, the more normal situation is for executive-inspired bills, which must be sponsored and introduced into the House and Senate by members, to be given some priority for consideration but also to be considered in detail in committees. They may be amended or even rejected, especially if the President does not have a majority of his party in control of the House and Senate. Even when this is the case, it is necessary to create and maintain bipartisan coalitions of support for most bills.

Congressional decline

Nevertheless, since the 1930s the executive has emerged as the prime initiator of legislation, with Congress becoming less of a positive force of influence on policy matters, though the Senate is still seen as a useful 'incubator' of new policy ideas often emanating from specific sub-committees. Congress, however, has become more than a law-making and fund-appropriating body.

As the national bureaucracy has grown in size, and expenditures have increased, House and Senate members have come to play an important if imperfectly understood role as scrutineers or overseers of this massive network of agencies, departments and commissions. In effect, they have become more and more concerned with activities which have a direct relationship with constituents or interests in their electoral districts or states. The 'decline' of Congress up to the 1970s was also a consequence of the fact that, as national governmental responsibilities increased, a single executive could make certain decisions more rapidly, if not more effectively, than 535 members of Congress.

Congressional change

The internal procedures of Congress consist of established rules and organisations, and informal practices. The former include the establishment of a permanent party leadership structure (Speaker – Majority Party Leader – Whip, and Minority Party Leader – Whip, in the House; Majority Party Leader – Whip, and Minority Party Leader – Whip in the Senate), a network of permanent standing committees, and the establishment of the seniority principle where length of continuous service is used to determine who chairs or obtains places on committees. The Speaker is a partisan figure presiding over House floor activities, and this position has at times been a very powerful one. Committee chairpersons are an alternative leadership group to the party leaders, but the erosion of the use of the seniority principle and other changes in committee activities have weakened the power of chairpersons. The House and Senate have changed in composition and in their priorities, and there have been structural adjustments in response to internal demands by members, as well as responses to the external political world, to new national and international issues, changes within the executive, and the demands of public opinion.

Congressional change in the 1970s

The 1970s witnessed a number of changes in the way in which Congress operates. Impetus for change was not only a response by the legislature to its marginalisation by the executive branch in the Vietnam and Watergate era, but also by a desire by many newer Congressmen to democratise its internal organisation.

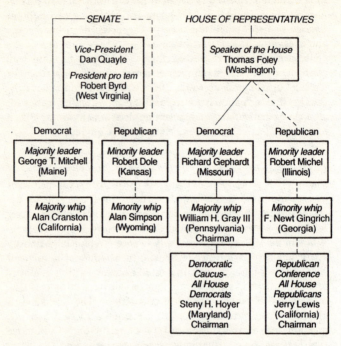

Figure 6.1. Party leaders in Congress (1989–90)

Further, the pace of reform and the desire for Congress to play a more active role in making and scrutinising public policy was accelerated by an influx of new members in that decade.

Changes in membership and career attitudes

1. Membership   Despite the fact that over 90 per cent of House members who seek re-election are returned, the so-called incumbency effect, the 1970s saw a rapid growth in new recruits. The high success rate of incumbents did conceal a high retirement rate which produced a Congress with much new blood. In 1974, 92 new members were elected, in 1976, 67; and in 1978, 77. By 1976 some 55 per cent of House members had been elected after 1970.

In the Senate in the 1970s comparisons in turnover are difficult, given that only one-third of the upper chamber retires every two years . But in the period 1972–76, 41 per cent of the Senate were in their freshman term. Until 1980 with the emergence of a Republican majority in the Senate, most of the replacement had been at the expense of senior Republicans.

Perhaps a more important change has been the long-term decline of Southern Democrats. In 1947 some 55 per cent of House Democrats represented Southern districts, but by 1977 this had halved to 28 per cent. This has also led to a lower proportion of Southerners holding committee chairs.

2. *Career attitudes* Building a career in the legislature has always been important for most members of the House and Senate. During the late nineteenth century the seniority system developed where members were rewarded for long service with committee chairs. Hence Representatives and Senators recognised the need to serve well those who elected them. In the 1970s as casework and constituency pressures increased, members of Congress voted funds to support large personal staffs, provide free mailing and travel privileges to ensure that constituents were kept informed of their Representatives' activities. Pressures of constituency work also have, in general, meant that more time is spent on maintaining links with the district and less time on legislative matters.

The defeat of leading Democratic Party Senators in the 1978 and 1980 elections, where opponents made great political capital from incumbents spending too much time in Washington, has led many to act more like their House colleagues in maintaining close links with the folks back home. The increase in constituency activity by both House and Senate members has meant a reduction in the time allocated to legislative responsibilities.

3. *Constituency–Congressional linkage* What the above evidence implies is that the appearance to constituents of a Representative or Senator may be of greater importance than how he or she works with colleagues in the House or Senate, on committees, in floor debate, or in the party caucus. Hence the 'home style', or perception of the member in the home district or state, can affect behaviour in the House or Senate and on committees. There has been an increase in individualistic behaviour in the Senate, and many Representatives have been diverted into preoccupation with the detail, as much as the substance and overall importance, of policy issues which come before them as bills. Thus, much effort is now expended in ensuring that individual interests are satisfied, and that everyone gets a share of the funds and programmes available. It is more difficult, therefore, to pass legislation which is redistributive in effect, concentrating financial or other resources on particular needs at the possible expense of others. Moreover, committee or sub-committee members considering requests from government and agencies will build up relationships with administrators which are cosy and mutually supportive, rather than critical or questioning.

Institutional changes in congressional-presidential relations

1. Financial and budgetary policy The financial controls held by Congress are jealously guarded, and there were important changes in the mid-1970s to strengthen the capacity of Congress to consider and change the budget presented annually by the executive. Within the House and Senate these matters were normally the responsibility of the House and Senate Appropriations Committees, who considered the different parts of the budget in important sub-committees. In the face of growing financial stringencies and constraints, and a deliberate attempt by the Nixon administration to challenge the authority of Congress to determine what should be spent, the Budget and Impoundment Control Act of 1974 set up a more coherent process in Congress to deal with the budget as a whole.

The Act established the following:

(*a*) House and Senate Budget Committees.

(*b*) The Congressional Budget Office to provide economic information and analysis to reduce dependence on the executive branch.

(*c*) New budget procedures and a detailed timetable for action on the budget.

(*d*) Prohibited presidential impoundment of funds unless both houses approve within forty-five days.

The budget process worked well for the first few years and Congress regained some capability to structure the budget as a whole. However, Congress did find it difficult to enact resolutions according to its own timetable. This problem became more severe under the Reagan administration as the President submitted budgets with large deficits. The President resisted tax increases to reduce the deficit and tried to reduce social welfare spending while simultaneously increasing military expenditure. Congress retaliated by reversing spending priorities but refused to propose a tax increase without presidential co-operation.

The result was the enactment of the Balanced Budget and Emergency Deficit Control Act 1985 (colloquially known as Gramm–Rudman–Hollings) which proposed drastic action to bring the federal budget into equilibrium (see Chapter 9).

The 1974 Act represents one of the strongest efforts made by Congress to control and enforce its constitutional functions. It also provided a reconciliation mechanism to overcome the decentralised committee system when making budget cuts in the Reagan era.

2. Foreign and defence policy   Changes have also taken place in the relative congressional and presidential influence over foreign policy. In 1972 Congress enacted legislation requiring all executive agreements completed by the President be sent to the House and Senate within sixty days of their signing. In addition, Congress has strengthened its influence in this arena by enacting:

(a) *The War Powers Resolution 1973*. Passed over President Nixon's veto, the resolution attempted to limit the President's ability to wage undeclared war. Under the Resolution the president must 'consult' with Congress in 'every possible instance' before involving US troops in hostilities. In addition the President is required to notify Congress within forty-eight hours of committing troops abroad and is prohibited from keeping troops there for more than sixty days without congressional approval. The President has, in addition, a further thirty days to withdraw troops.

The Mayaguez incident in 1975 indicates that the President is able to exclude Congress from the decision-making process, while other critics have suggested the Resolution allows the President to wage unlimited war for sixty days at the end of which period Congress may find it difficult to force the President to bring the troops home.

(b) *The Arms Control Export Act 1976*. This enables Congress to veto all arms sales over $25 million.

(c) *The Nuclear Non-Proliferation Act 1978*. This enables

Congress to veto executive decisions on the export of nuclear fuels and technology.

Overall the executive branch's control over the information required for any effective decision-making gives it the edge over Congress in foreign and defence policy. This imbalance cannot be righted by improving staffing and information systems. While the primary source of foreign and defence intelligence remains in the executive branch the legislature will find it difficult to play a major role in the determination of such policies.

Internal reforms

The committee system and the seniority system which traditionally determined the leadership of congressional committees came under attack in the 1970s. The demand for reform came particularly from comparatively junior Democratic Party members of the House who felt that their influence on policy making would be minimal, given the domination of the committee system by old and sometimes autocratic chairs who held office by dint of continuous service in the House. The election in 1974 of seventy-five new Democrats, the 'Watergate babies', provided the impetus for change.

1. The Democratic caucus During the 1970s the Democratic caucus emerged as a major force in the House both as an instigator of the reforms that changed the structure of the House and an important check on the independent committee chairs and the seniority system. These reforms included:

(a) *The effective abolition of seniority (1971).* The Democratic caucus agreed that House committee chairs would be elected by secret ballot if 20 per cent of members so requested.

(b) *No member could be chair of more than one legislative sub-committee (1971).* This made it possible for younger liberal and non-Southern members to become sub-committee chairpersons.

(c) *Adoption of the Sub-Committee Bill of Rights (1973).* This created in each House committee and mini-Democratic caucus with the authority to elect chairpersons and redistribute committee powers of staffing, scheduling and agenda setting to sub-committees.

(d) *Strengthening of sub-committeess (1974).* Most committees should establish at least four sub-committees and the chair and ranking minority member be allowed to have one staff aide.

(e) In 1975 the Democratic caucus ousted three senior committee chairmen, Wright Patman (Banking), W. R. Poage (Agriculture), and F. E. Hebert (Armed Services).

These *party* reforms weakened the old seniority system under which committee chairpersons and members had been appointed. They opened up the committee process so that most standing committee work is conducted in public while the Sub-Committee Bill of Rights gave sub-committees a permanent staff of their own and permanent responsibilities.

2. Legislative Reorganization Act 1970   The passage of this act constituted a landmark for Congress and was the catalyst for further change later in the decade. The Act had three main provisions:

(a) It instituted an electronic voting system which made public, for the first time, how House and Senate members voted.

(b) It increased the number of professional staff for each committee, and permitted them to hire consultants.

(c) It required House and Senate committees to issue over-sight reports every two years.

The consequences of this legislation were far-reaching. Both the number of roll-call votes increased as did the number of members voting, conscious that their own constituents could now keep track of their representatives' activities in Washington. This in turn led many Congressmen to pay more attention to public opinion back home. The second effect was the beginning of the professionalisation of the committee system to cope with the increasing complexity of legislation and make Congress less dependent on the executive branch for information.

3. House committee reforms   In 1973-74 a bipartisan committee headed by Richard Bolling (Democrat, Missouri) studied the problems of House committee reform, especially some of the key standing committees such as the Ways and Means Committee, which had massive responsibilities for taxation and other 'financial' matters. The Bolling committee recommended that there should be 15 exclusive, important standing committees and 7 non-exclusive, and it attempted to improve coherence of responsibilities and equality of workload. However, there was strong opposition to many of the proposals, especially in the Democratic Party caucus, and in the end there were many modifications made to the original proposals. Even so, some jurisdictional tidying-up was approved, and the Speaker's power of referring bills to committees was made stronger, including the power to create *ad hoc* committees to consider complicated bills. However, the committee structure still contained serious weaknesses, and a new reform committee was set up in 1979 to make recommendations on committee reorganisation, but few significant changes were made.

4. Senate committee reforms These were much more successful. A committee chaired by Senator Stevenson from Illinois was set up in 1976 to look at, and make recommendations for change in, the existing committee structure; it reported in 1977. In contrast to the House, the Senate was prepared to consider major changes, including the cutting of the number of committees from 31 to 15, the consolidation of jurisdictions for complex issues such as energy, and the establishment of responsibilities for oversight or scrutiny of policy by committees. Senior Senators chairing major committees were placated, and individual Senators were limited with respect to sub-committee assignments. The overall changes improved the working environment of the Senate. The Senate innovations were more far reaching than those of the House, partly because the Senate committees are not as significant in terms of decision making as those in the House. Senators are less specialised in their committee work and policy concerns, while the House is larger and has stricter procedures governing debate of bills on the floor, and so individual members have less opportunity of exercising influence outside the committees of which they are members.

5. Expanding staff resources The number of congressional staff members has risen dramtically in recent years as Table 6.1 illustrates. This growth has been in both personal and committee staffs, and can be explained by the increasing workload of Congress, the complexity of issues, increasing competition among committees and members, the election of activist members, the

Table 6.1 Number of congressional staff members 1957–80

	Senate		House	
	Committee	*Personal*	*Committee*	*Personal*
1957	558	1,115	375	2,441
1967	621	1,749	589	4,005
1972	918	2,426	783	5,280
1976	1,534	3,251	1,548	6,939
1978	1,151	3,268	1,844	6,295
1980	1,108	4,281	1,918	8,667

diffusion of power, constituency service, and legislative–executive conflict.

(*a*) *Personal staff*. Each House member in 1980 was allowed to hire 18 full-time and 4 part-time employees, while a Senator's personal staff averaged 35. Recent evidence suggests that Congressmen's personal staff are fundamentally concerned with their members' re-election. Most House and Senate members have an office in their district or state where by 1980 some 2,500 of their staff were based.

(*b*) *Committee staff*. With the expansion of sub-committee activity has come the growth of committee staff. Although staff functions differ from committee to committee, they are generally policy specialists who help committees develop and evaluate policies, suggest alternatives to legislation, advise members how to vote and oversee the administration of legislation.

In addition to the growth in personal and committee staff, Congress enhanced its own research and information base through the development of various support agencies.

(*a*) *Congressional Research Service (CRS)*. This was established by the Legislative Reorganization Act 1970 to meet the need for independent policy advice and information by committees and individual members.

(*b*) *General Accounting Office (GAO)*. Congress's main auditor and programme investigator, it is specifically required to review executive department programmes in terms of efficiency and economy. In 1981 it concluded that many weapons systems fail because of 'overtly complex designs and the lack of attention to the abilities of the troops who use them in the field'.

(*c*) *Office of Technology Assessment (OTA).* Created to provide Congress with scientific and technical support for members and committees, its primary mandate is to conduct long-term studies of the social, biological, physical, economic and political effect of technology.

(*d*) *Congressional Budget Office (CBO).* Established by the Budget and Impoundment Control Act 1974, this is Congress's answer to the OMB and CEA. It provides an independent assessment and analysis of the President's budget for the House and Senate Budget Committee.

The cumulative effect of these changes in both the House and Senate has been both a strengthening and a fragmentation of the legislature. The strengthening can be seen in the increase in personal and committee staffs in addition to the creation of four new congressional organisations – CRS, GAO, OTA and CBO. The fragmentation through the development of sub-committee government inside the Congress, and outside, rise in importance of constituency service. This has led one writer to suggest that the United States now has two Congresses.

Two Congresses

Roger Davidson has identified two 'distinct, yet inextricably bound' Congresses. The first is Congress the united political institution, the House and Senate performing their constitutional obligations and considering legislation. The second is the Congress which consists of the individual members – 435 Representatives and 100 Senators – who are elected by voters across the country, and who depend on those voters for re-election. There is also, in effect, a third Congress: two rival institutions in the legislative process. So Congress is at one and the same time a pair of political institutions who, in co-operation and competition, perform a variety of activities, make decisions on legislation, appropriate money and check on the bureaucracy, and two representative popular assemblies of individuals representing a diverse range of relatively parochial interests. This is the paradox of the modern Congress – concerned daily with major items of legislation which are often complex in nature, yet with a structure which permits the individual members to determine how and to what purpose the constitutional responsibilities of Congress will be used. As a result, Congress is better equipped to satisfy the particular interests of constitutents and special interests than to provide a coherent and cohesive legislative response to the problems of the nation. The weak nature of party leadership within Congress does not help this situation.

Legislative–executive relations in the post-reform era

The internal reforms of Congress, the turnover of members and a changed attitude of Congressmen have had an impact on presidential–congressional relationships. The attitude that one branch has towards the other has a crucial effect on public policy in both a specific and general sense. The post-Vietnam and Watergate Congresses were more assertive in both domestic and foreign policy arenas. Even the Reagan presidency, in the long run, did not see a return to the imperial presidency of the 1960s.

Domestic policy

In the 1970s Congress sought to defend many of the Great Society programmes passed in the previous Johnson presidency against executive attempts to deny the funds. The 1980s, after the initial Reagan budget success, saw Congress take action to protect many social security programmes.

The Senate, too, through its 'advise and consent' powers, began to critically evaluate presidential appointees for posts in the executive branch and for the Supreme Court. Examples abound, from Jimmy Carter's Budget Director Bert Lance, through to George Bush's Secretary for Defense John Tower. The Senate conducted thorough investigations as to the suitability of nominees for high office.

However, initially, the consequences of more sub-committees, more professional staff and research aids, more open procedures in committees and a strengthening of party organisation and controls did not appear to have improved the capacity of Congress to develop coherent policy programmes or respond to presidential initiatives in an unified manner. By the mid-1980s Congress made a series of attempts to provide coherent policy options in a number of issue areas, on the budget and foreign trade, for example. The trade bill debated in 1987 is an indication of how difficult it is for Congress to act in a single-minded manner, for so many amendments were added to appease constituency interests, to ensure passage, that the main thrust of the legislation was lost.

The problem remains, that in spite of enhanced constitutional and personal resources, in addition to constituency pressures, Congress and Congressmen find it difficult to be pro-active in making domestic public policy.

Foreign and defence policy

Beginning with the War Powers Act which sought to give Congress influence over presidential decisions to commit US troops abroad, Congress began to exercise more control over foreign policy matters. The Jackson amendment in 1974 attempted to link an improvement in US–USSR trade relations to relaxing the emigration restrictions on Soviet Jews. Other amendments have prohibited arms sales or aid to specific countries, or subjected such decisions to possible veto by Congress through concurrent resolutions which require a majority in both House and Senate.

The Senate has become more sensitive about the ratification of treaties. It only agreed to the Panama Canal treaties in 1978 by one vote and put on ice President Carter's SALT II arms-control measure.

The return of the Senate to Republican control in 1981 did not mean that President Reagan had an easier ride in dealing with Congress on the detail of foreign policy. Often specific foreign policy issues have attracted the attention of interst groups, for example, the sale of early warning aircraft to Saudi Arabia which attracted the opposition of the Jewish lobby. This constituency interest has also led the House Foreign Affairs Committee to become more active in the scrutiny and oversight of foreign policy. In June 1986 in a debate on Nicaragua, wary of the United States becoming involved in an undeclared war, the House added provisions to a bill limiting the deployment of US servicemen in the war zone.

Since 1986, with the return of Democratic Party control in the Senate, the upper chamber has been more active in foreign and defence policy. Sam Nunn, Chair of the Armed Services Committee in 1987, began an attack on President Reagan's interpretation of the 1972 ABM Treaty which the President argued would allow the testing and development of the Star Wars programme. Some scholars have suggested that the Senate's narrower view, which precluded this, led the President into negotiations with the Soviet Union over arms control and enabled him to conclude the INF Treaty which was ratified by the Senate.

Executive–legislative conflict over foreign policy can produce unpredictability, with foreign countries uncertain as to whether executive actions will be supported or sustained by Congress. The influence that Congress has had in recent years has been through oversight and patient negotiations with the executive branch, but in the final analysis the weapons it has at its disposal to enforce its views are blunt, and include the cutting of funds, vetoing a particular decision or rejecting or amending treaties which have been negotiated over many years.

Presidential policies and Congress

Presidents normally have problems in getting their policy initiatives accepted by Congress. Part of the reason for this is the complex procedure by which the House and Senate consider bills, reach a final compromise version, and then, through a separate appropriations process, provide funds to permit the implementation of the new law. In this process there are many opportunities for individual members or groups of members to amend the bill, and for outside interest groups to lobby against the bill. Another factor is the low level of party loyalty reflecting in voting in the House and Senate. Party loyalty has declined to such an extent that since 1946 the proportion of votes where there has been strict partisan division has not been above 10 per cent in any year. These factors mean that if a President wished to be successful with a policy he needs to persuade sufficient members of the House and Senate, irrespective of party, that it is in their interests to support his legislation.

All this does not mean that Congress does not have the capacity to initiate legislation, simply that as a policy-making body it is inevitably less cohesive, and so less effective, than the executive. The Congress as well as the President possesses the capacity to initiate or to veto major policy changes. Hence the normal pattern is for compromise and limited change. In this sense the fact that the Congress is a representative institution means that whether it goes along with the President or challenges executive initiatives depends entirely on the attitudes of its members.

Oversight of the bureaucracy

An important feature of the modern Congress is the large number of staff available to committees and sub-committees. Among other things this has increased the interest of members and subcommittees in scrutinising and overseeing the implementation of programmes by federal agencies and departments. Such oversight has expanded considerably as active 'entrepreneurial' staff seek out particular issues to scrutinise, and agency and department officials are now required to testify at special oversight hearings. Such oversight is both necessary and proper and is very popular with members of Congress. Given the size of the federal bureaucracy, and public demands to cut governmental spending, such scrutiny could have important consequences. However, despite the massive information and staff resources, congressional oversight too often reflects the particular concerns of individuals or groups in Congress. Other mechanisms such as 'sunset' laws, which seek to sift out on a regular basis programmes which are no longer viable, need to be applied by members who have no vested interest in protecting the agencies or departments implementing these programmes. The difficulty here again is that members of Congress are too often concerned with protecting programmes which may have the support of special interests who could affect their election chances, rather than engaging in comprehensive and critical scrutiny. The new information and staff supports are used as much to sustain individual concerns as to strengthen the capacity of Congress as a whole to make laws, oversee the bureaucracy or formulate policy alternatives.

Congress in the 1980s

Congressional-presidential relations 1980–89

The election of Ronald Reagan in 1980, and with him a Republican majority in the Senate for the first time in 25 years, had a great impact on congressional behaviour. The House remained in Democratic Party control, but with a Republican Senate and President, many Democrats wondered whether this was the beginning of a conservative realignment in American politics. This uncertainty aided President Reagan in achieving important victories in Congress in 1981 for his budget and tax-policy initiatives. He was helped not only by a high level of Republican Party unity in the House, but he was also able to attract sufficient numbers of conservative Democrats to his cause.

As the 1982 mid-term elections approached, the bipartisan support that Reagan developed in Congress began to decline, as conservative Democrats and Northern moderate Republicans became less loyal to the President. Following the election, in which the Democrats focused on the President's handling of the economy as the central issue, the Democrats gained 26 seats in the Houe but the Republicans retained their majority in the Senate. This meant that Reagan had to modify some of his demands and seek particular and new coalitions of support in Congress. He proved skilful in getting such support when he really needed it, but there were reactions in the House to the work of agencies such as the Environmental Protection Agency and the Department of the Interior. Oversight investigations were conducted, with the President trying to claim executive privilege to avoid disclosing certain evidence. The general situation was changed in 1983 when the Supreme Court declared unconstitutional certain types of veto provisions included in legislation by Congress. This is the latest development in the continuing struggle to establish a new balance between executive and administrative authority and controls by Congress.

The 1984 congressional elections saw the Republicans gain 15 seats in the House (and still remain the minority party) while retaining a comfortable majority in the Senate. Despite Republican gains in the House, Congress did not shift ideologically to the right. On the contrary, Congress began to challenge many of the President's programmes. On the federal budget, Gramm–Rudman–Hollings targets (see p. 137), which were designed to reduce the deficit in 1986, Congress decided to cut only $11.7 billion, but excluded some sensitive programmes like social security, aid for the poor and Reagan's Strategic Defense Initiative. The funding of Star Wars and aid to the Contras was reduced in 1986, and also Congress overrode the President's veto on sanctions to South Africa. By the time of the 1986 mid-term elections Reagan's relationship with Congress was much more strained, as the legislature began to assert itself against the President.

In the ensuing congressional elections the Democrats regained control of the Senate for the first time since 1980 as well as increasing their majority in the House of Representatives. For the last two years of his presidency Reagan was faced by a Congress in which both Houses were controlled by the Democrats: a

Democratic Congress that behaved responsibly and, in the run up to the presidential elections of 1988, began to assert its authority.

The size of the budget remained the major political issue as the Democrats began to question the level of defence spending, particularly for Star Wars and for aid to the Contras. The only issue which pushed financial matters off the front page and which dominated the political agenda into 1988 was the revelation that the Reagan administration had supplied arms to Iran in return for the release of US hostages held in the Lebanon and had channelled some of the revenue from this transaction to the Nicaraguan Contras. These revelations led to the resignation of the Chairman of the National Security Council, Admiral Poindexter, and the dismissal of the man who allegedly organised the affair, Lieutenant-Colonel North. Special Prosecutor Lawrence Walsh was appointed by the President to diffuse the congressional investigation.

The President also suffered defeats on the domestic front. There was the failure to get his nomination for a vacant Supreme Court seat, Robert Bork, confirmed by the Senate, while another withdrew after revelations about drug abuse. Finally Judge David Kennedy was confirmed. Throughout 1988 there were revelations about the integrity of many appointees in the Reagan administration. Over a hundred had left under a cloud, and finally a close Reagan friend, Ed Meese, the Attorney-General, was forced to resign after a congressional investigation.

The Democrats in Congress from 1986 to 1988 used the legislature to slowly challenge the Reagan administration which they saw as vulnerable on a series of issues, and with 'Irangate' saw parallels with the Watergate scandal of the Nixon era.

The first months of the Bush presidency have seen a continuation of congressional reassertiveness. Although the President had achieved some success with Congress on the Nicaraguan Contras and sent a new budget to Capitol Hill, these have been overshadowed by the defeat of John Tower, his nominee for Secretary of Defense.

2. Congressional workload in the 1980s   The decade was dominated by financial, budgetary and economic policy issues. This will continue as long as the federal budget deficit and trade deficit remains high and these matters put a severe strain on those responsible for implementing the congressional budgetary process. That members of Congress are more conscious of the need to deal with overall economic issues was evidenced by the quick passage of the Gramm–Rudman–Hollings Act in 1985, which would allow Congress to make hard choices when it came to budget cuts. Furthermore, from 1980 to 1986 it was more difficult to get agreement between the House and Senate, given divided party control.

Since 1986, with Congress controlled by the Democrats, the legislature has become more partisan and less consensual on economic matters. Budgets reflect Democratic Congressmen's concerns with maintaining social welfare programmes and with reducing the proportion of the budget spent on defence. In addition, Democrats concerned with the growing trade imbalance enacted a Bill to protect US industry, which was vetoed by the President. The Bush presidency will continue to see tension on economic matters with Congress.

3. In both the House and Senate, members are pressured by well-established labour or business interests, but also by new public-interest groups and sectional groups concerned with issues such as the government, equal rights for women or abortion. Pressure is being exerted by conservative Republicans, especially in the Senate, for new legislation on constitutional amendments relating to social issues, like abortion and school prayers, and for a balanced budget requirement. With the Gramm–Rudman–Hollings Act they have achieved this last goal but on other issues have made little progress.

Conclusion

The paradox of the modern Congress is that both branches possess advantages and attributes which most other legislatures lack. These ought to strengthen the capacity of Congress to exercise an independent influence on the policy outputs of government in Washington. However, the effect of the recent reforms has been one of marginally improving the ability to take coherent action for the common good, while increasing the opportunities for individuals to be influential through sub-committee work, or for scrutiny of particular aspects of administration, and thus accelerating a trend towards the diffusion and decentralisation of decision-making. It is therefore not surprising to learn that citizens see their own Representatives and Senators in a more favourable light than the overall performance of Congress. House and Senate members have permanent offices and personal staff which help them to be independent careerists, and their electoral fortunes are often only loosely linked with those of their party. Not all behaviour in Congress is conditioned by self-interest or the perceived concerns of constituents, but the commitment to develop coherent public policy, co-ordinate government and ensure that administrators implement legislation effectively and efficiently, remains weak. Congressional change in the future will continue to depend on the concerns and instincts of members; only constitutional reform and changes in party influences will change the principal emphasis on individualism.

Further reading

C. J. Bailey, *The U.S. Congress*, Blackwell, 1989.
R. F. Fenno, Jr, *Congressmen in Committees*, Little, Brown, 1973.
R. F. Fenno, Jr, *Home Style*, Little, Brown, 1978.
A. Maass, *Congress and the Common Good*, Basic Books, 1983.
W. J. Oleszek, *Congressional Procedures and the Policy Process*, Congressional Quarterly Press, 2nd edn, 1984.

Questions

1. What are the important differences between the Senate and the House of Representatives?

2. What are the defects and advantages of the increased importance of sub-committees in the House and Senate?

3. Why has recent congressional reform been seen as a mixed blessing?

7

POLITICAL PARTIES

Introduction

A common theme among students of American politics today is that political parties are in a state of decline. However, there is no consensus as to why political parties have fallen on such hard times. Some observers note the alleged decline in public support for the party system. They argue that there has been, in recent decades, a decline in partisan loyalty and a decline in interest in elections and voting among the electorate. Linked to this view, a second group of scholars suggest that parties have declined as organisations. The rise of candidate-centred presidential politics and the importance of the mass media as transmitters of political information are illustrations of the trend away from parties organising politics to newer institutions performing the traditional functions of political parties.

Whatever evidence is presented to support the argument that parties are in a state of decline, there is one underlying theme – that parties are less relevant as political institutions in American society today. This implies that parties were once highly regarded in the political culture. However, an analysis of the origin and development of American political parties suggests that they have always been regarded with suspicion, but as an indispensable evil to provide some integrating mechanism to a nation with a divided political structure created by the Constitution.

The origins and development of the party system

The Constitution, which established a balanced machinery for the organisation of government and provided mechanisms for the election of the President and members of Congress, makes no mention of political parties. Political parties or 'factions' were seen by many of the Founding Fathers as being nationally divisive and, in the words of James Madison, as 'dangerous organisations that needed to be discouraged and controlled'. Yet within a short time the new nation was divided into two camps, the Federalists and anti-Federalists, in the campaign for the ratification of the new Constitution.

The divisions in American society over ratification did not lead immediately to the formation of political parties. But, by the end of the eighteenth century, differences had begun to occur in the political elite, particularly between Hamilton and Jefferson, firstly over the role of the federal government and its programme for dealing with the economic problems of the new nation, and secondly over governmental attitudes towards the French Revolution. These conflicts over economic and foreign policy raised serious questions concerning what interests and sectors of society should be regulated, protected and benefited. Hence conflict among the political elite on these issues, and the link between these issues and varied socio-economic interests, provided the seed-bed for the origin of political parties. Thus by 1800 the first national parties, the Federalists and Republicans, were organised in Congress. Although there were no national party organisations, party tickets or use of party symbols, as we understand them today, both Alexander Hamilton's supporters, the Federalists, and Thomas Jefferson's Democratic-Republicans, concentrated on supporting partisan candidates for Congress and the presidency. The development of party organisations in the states came later, and the more socially and economically diverse the state, the more advanced its party development.

Why did parties emerge at this time? Political historian William Chambers suggests four reasons:

(a) *Diversity of society*: the development of a varied and complex political, social and economic society generated rivalry which promoted party development.

(b) *Decline of deference politics*: the emergence and promise of a democratic political system, combined with social and economic change, weakened social and political deference.

(c) *A common political arena*: the Constitution established a federal government with national powers which provided colonial politicians with a national political arena conducive to national party politics.

(d) *The political elites needed a political vehicle*: parties provided political leaders with an organisation through which they could conduct politics in a businesslike manner.

However, the politicians who organised the first political parties did not do so because they believed in democracy. They realised that the Constitution fragmented political power within and among the institutions of government and saw parties as a mechanism for organising political choices, diffusing conflict and making compromises possible. Secondly, the political elite realised that public support was necessary to legitimise their activities and sought to win this support by influencing and expanding electorate and appealing to the increasing diverse group interests in the nation.

Since the ratification of the Constitution, the United States has had five national party systems, or periods where two or more parties compete for power in government and for the support of the electorate, and over a dozen significant third parties. The current party system dates from the election of Franklin Roosevelt in 1932 and was brought about by the economic crisis which followed the Great Crash of 1929. Between 1932 and 1964 the Democratic Party won seven of the nine presidential elections, occupying the White House for twenty-eight years; it also controlled both the House of Representatives and the Senate for all but four of these years.

However, the success of the Republican Party in winning five of the six presidential contests since 1968 has led many political commentators to suggest that the United States is entering another period of party realignment from which the Republicans may well emerge as the majority party. A Republican Party majority in the US Senate from 1981 to 1987 gave further support to this claim.

The United States: a two-party system?

An analysis of the development of political parties, since the establishment of the first party system in the late eighteenth century, reveals that two major parties have dominated political life. The Democratic Party has endured since Jefferson's presidency in one form or another, and in successive eras has been challenged by the Federalist, Whig and Republican Parties. With few exceptions, as Allan Sindler has noted, the Democrats and

Republicans 'persistently poll over 90% of the national popular vote' and 'there has been little multipartyism'.

Third parties

There have been significant third parties which have been active in American presidential politics:

Third party movements have included:

(*a*) 1892 *Populist Party*, polling 8.5 per cent of the popular vote.

(*b*) 1912 *Roosevelt Progressive Party*, polling 27.4 per cent of the popular vote.

(*c*) 1924 *La Follette Progressive Party*, polling 16.6 per cent of the popular vote.

(*d*) 1968 George Wallace's American Independent Party, polling 13.5 per cent of the popular vote.

(*e*) 1980 *John Anderson's Independent Party*, polling 7 per cent of the popular vote.

Third parties have usually served as temporary resting places for dissatisfied groups of voters who have broken away from one of the major parties and who are perhaps in transit to another. Third parties, too, have rarely won enough votes to threaten the two major parties but Roosevelt's Progressive Party in 1912 and George Wallace's American Independent Party in 1968 came close to affecting the outcome of the presidential election.

A common tendency among third parties is that they have been formed and led by disgruntled leaders from one of the major parties who have left because of political differences with their former friends.

Minor Parties

Apart from the 'major' third parties, every presidential election has a number of small parties offering candidates for the presidency. For example, the Socialist Party and the Prohibition Party have appeared regularly on ballot papers in the last fifty years, and in 1984 fourteen minor parties pooled just over half a million votes, with David Bergland of the Libertarian Party attracting half of these. These parties accept that they are unlikely to achieve electoral success and stand for election to promote a single principle, as with the Prohibition Party, for a specific ideological philosophy, as with Bergland's Libertarian Party.

Why a two-party system?

The American political system has been dominated for most of its history by two major parties; the question arises why this is so, given the sectional, class and social divisions that exist in the nation. Among the explanations which have been offered are:

Institutional and electoral factors

From a constitutional perspective the presidency is the focal point of political life. A single nationally elected executive, the main prize in politics, can only be won by a party that can build a coalition of voters to support one man. This necessitates parties building organisations and drawing support for their candidate across the nation. Once this electoral coalition has been achieved, a party is placed in an advantageous position and usually capitalises by dominating presidential election contests for several decades. The Roosevelt and Truman years provide a good example of this. Conversely, parties which are unable to build a national electoral constituency or which are regionally based, for example George Wallace's American Independent Party, will have little chance of winning the presidency.

Historical factors

The debate over the ratification of the Constitution divided the nation into two groups, and this division or duality of interest has sustained the two-party system. V. O. Key (in *Politics, Parties and Pressure Groups*, Crowell, 5th edn, 1964) has suggested that the initial conflict between financial and commercial interests and the interests of the agricultural sector fostered the two-party system, and these rivalries were later replaced by the North–South conflict over the issue of slavery, which in turn was supplemented by the socio-economic divisions of the present party system into Democrats and Republicans (see Chapter 11). As Frank Sorauf argues, this argument can be sustained by the natural dualism of politics: the party in power versus party out of power, government versus opposition, which reduce political contests to two camps and which give rise to two political parties.

Political socialisation and patterns of belief

While institutional and electoral reasons force party politics into a two-way mode, the question remains: why do the *same* two parties reappear at election after election? Historically they have not, with the first party system having the Federalists challenging the Democratic-Republicans, later the Whigs fought the Democrats, and by the Civil War the Republicans and Democrats emerged as the major parties, but with party divisions different from those of today. If this is the case, why then do the Democratic and Republican Parties still persist? The answer is through the process of political socialisation, where party allegiance is passed on from generation to generation (see Chapter 11). Democrats and Republicans have been structuring voter choice for so long that challenges from new parties are difficult. The current party cleavage emerged during the New Deal and is based broadly on the economic divisions of the time.

None of these factors exclusively account for the development and maintenance of the two-party system. Rather it is a combination of the three. Reinforcing these explanations is a consensus on the basis beliefs and values which underly the political system. Americans generally have a high regard for the Constitution and for their political institutions (although not necessarily for the politicians who operate these institutions), and support a regulated and free market economy. A majority of the electorate do not identify with political extremes and see themselves standing near the middle ground of politics. When political parties have nominated presidential candidates who have been perceived as representing extreme opinions, as did the Republicans with Barry Goldwater in 1964, and the Democrats with George McGovern in 1972, they have been badly defeated at the polls.

A two-party system in reality?

Recent presidential election contests indicate that the Republicans and Democrats compete strongly for the White House. Since 1952 the Republicans have had an advantage, winning the office seven times in ten elections. But does the close rivalry between the parties for the White House conceal a more complex picture of party competition for other electoral offices?

Parties in Congress
Despite recent Republican domination of presidential politics, with election victories for Dwight Eisenhower, Richard Nixon,

Table 7.1   Party divisions in Congress 1964–88

| | House of Representatives | | Senate | |
	Dem.	Rep.	Dem.	Rep.
1964	295	140	68	32
1968	243	192	58	42
1972	242	192	56	42
1976	292	143	61	38
1980	243	192	46	53
1982	269	166	45	55
1984	253	182	47	53
1986	260	175	54	46
1988	262	173	55	45

Totals of less than 435 or 100 in the House and Senate after 1964 indicate other parties or independents.

Ronald Reagan and George Bush, the Democratic Party has, since 1932, had a commanding control of Congress. In the House of Representatives the Republicans have only been in a majority for four years, 1947–49 and 1953–55. In the Senate, however, the Republicans have been more successful, controlling the upper chamber for a total of ten years, 1947–49, 1953–55, 1981–87. As Table 7.1 indicates, Democratic majorities, when the party has controlled Congress, have been substantial, particularly in the House, where since 1960 its majority has never been below 50. In the Senate the Republicans have again been the minority party, but in 1978 began to challenge Democratic hegemony, gaining seats in the mid-term elections, and by 1980 they became the majority party in the upper chamber. By 1984 the Republican dream of dominating both houses of Congress still remained unfulfilled. While the Republicans controlled the Senate, a majority in the House still eluded them. For, despite Reagan's personal popularity, the GOP was unable to translate his personal support into votes for its candidates for the legislature. This point was reinforced by the 1986 mid-term elections where the Democrats regained control of the Senate.

A further Republican presidential victory in 1988 still saw continued Democratic Party control of both the House and Senate, which has led some commentators to suggest that a two-party system does not exist in Congress, but that the legislature has a 'one party dominant' system in which the Democrats almost continually outnumber their Republican opponents. The data presented in Table 7.1 tends to support this view.

An alternative interpretation of the parties in Congress has been advanced by James McGregor Burns. He argues that both the Democratic and Republican parties in Congress can be divided into a presidential and a congressional faction. Thus Congress has a 'four-party' system. Presidential Democrats seek support from the major urban areas of the nation, and tend to be more liberal and supportive of activist and Progressive Democratic Party Presidents. Congressional Democrats are based in the rural areas, are more conservative, and work closely with congressional Republicans to form a conservative coalition which on significant occasions in recent years has had great influence in Congress. Presidential Republicans differ in a similar way from their congressional party colleagues. The former represent mainly Eastern suburban districts, and are more liberal, while the latter are Western, rurally based and conservative. Conflict between the two wings of each party may be more bitter than disputes between the parties, each wing seeking to impose its ideals on their colleagues. The Goldwater presidential candidacy in 1964 illustrates the success that Congressional Republicans had in imposing their candidate for the White House on the presidential Republicans. His subsequent defeat indicated that the Republican Party needed not only conservative support in the country but broader electoral coalition. The election of Ronald Reagan and George Bush to the White House in the 1980s suggests perhaps that the conservative congressional Republicans are now in the ascendancy.

A third party division could be made in both Houses of Congress – between the liberal and conservative factions of both parties. This returns to the idea of a two-party system, but a system based on ideology and not party allegiance. The liberal wings of both parties combine, often, to support a President who believes that the federal government should play an activist role in society; to maintain full employment and provide for the social welfare of the American people, Conservatives, on the other hand, think that many of the problems facing the United States have been caused by too much federal government intervention, and believe that individuals should be left to resolve their own problems. President Reagan's success in the first year of his presidency in persuading Congress to accept his budget provides an illustration of the 'conservative' coalition in operation – a coalition of Republicans and Southern Democrats. In 1985 this coalition won nearly 90 per cent of the times it appeared – indicating that on some issues the ideological differences in Congress, irrespective of party, are more finely balanced.

When looking at Congress, it may appear that the Democratic Party has dominated for much of the time since 1932, but behind party labels voting alliances are more complex and are based on factors other than party allegiance.

Party competition in the United States

The nature of the party system in each of the fifty states again illustrates how misleading it is to describe the United States as having a competitive two-party system. Until the mid-1970s only 23 states could be thus defined. Of the remainder, seven states were overwhelmingly dominated by the Democratic Party, particularly in the South where the Republican Party rarely achieved political office. In recent years, however, following success for the Republican Party at the presidential level, GOP strength has been growing in the Southern Democratic heartlands. In 1986 the Republicans won five governorships in the South and in 1988 James Martin was re-elected in North Carolina. These victories are important for the patronage that goes with such offices, they should aid the Republicans in building strong state parties and are also a step towards capturing state legislatures in 1990 which will control congressional re-districting following the census.

The Democratic and Republican parties may compete on almost even terms for the presidency, but in Congress and in the fifty states, party competition is more complex. In Congress, although the Democratic Party dominates, the conservative–liberal ideological cleavage is finely balanced. In the fifty states, there are still many which are dominated by a single party, but in recent elections, even though the Republican Party has maintained a strong challenge in governors' races, in 1984 the Democrats still controlled 65 per cent of the state legislatures.

Party organisation and membership

The organisational structure of American parties could be depicted as a pyramid (see Fig. 7.1) with the National Committee

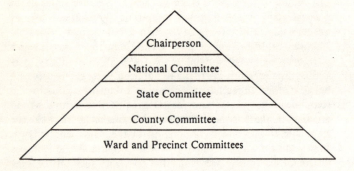

Figure 7.1 The party organisation

and its chairperson at the top, and with state and local party
organisations ranked below.

National party organisation

The national committee

The pinnacle of party structure is the national committee. This is
composed of party officials representing each state, and including
the chair of each state party organisation. Currently the Republican National Committee (RNC) has over 150 members while the
Democratic National Committee (DNC) totals 350. The
chairperson of each national committee is chosen by the parties'

presidential nominee and prospers or fades into obscurity depending on the nominee's success. In 1988, following the defeat of Richard Dukakis, DNC chair Paul Kirk resigned, to be replaced by Ron Brown, Jesse Jackson's campaign manager in 1988.

National committees have little power. They plan and organise the parties' quadrennial conventions and between these act as a limited source of ideas and information for the state party organisations. With the advent of extra-party, candidate-centred presidential campaign organisation, national party committees do not control presidential election campaigns. In 1972 Richard Nixon's re-election campaign was spearheaded by CREEP, while in 1988 the George Bush campaign team was organised by James Baker. Often, as with Jimmy Carter in 1976 and 1980, the national committee was ignored when campaign strategy was planned and organised.

Although national committees may appear to have a limited role in organising elections, in the 1970s both the DNC and RNC began to expand their activities.

1. Democratic National Committee Following the 1968 convention the party established the McGovern–Fraser Commission to consider party reforms. In its final report, the commission suggested rule changes to open the party to greater participation by women, minorities and youth in an attempt to weaken control by local party organisations over the selection of convention delegates. In 1972, the DNC threatened to deny representation to any state delegation which did not comply with the new rules, and did unseat the Chicago Democrats led by Mayor Daley. Through such procedural reforms the DNC successfully began to exert control over state parties in an attempt to create a national party organisation.

2. Republican National Committee In the 1970s the Republicans did little to open up the delegate selection process. Instead it concentrated on organisational reform. From 1976, under the full-time chairmanship of William Brock, the party strengthened its fund-raising capability, conducted election analyses, launched a research service and advised candidates running for political office. The effectiveness of these organisational changes were seen with the successful co-ordinated Republican challenge to gain control of the presidency and a majority in the Senate at the 1980 elections.

National convention
Every four years each party meets to nominate its candidate for the presidency. The national convention is the supreme governing body of the party. It determines party policy, decides on party rules and establishes the national committee to organise the party until the next convention. In recent years the party convention usually endorses its nominee for the presidency: its policy-making role is almost non-existent, this being determined by the parties' candidate for the presidency.

Congressional campaign organisation
Both parties in both the House and Senate have established campaign committees to assist in the re-election of party members to Congress. The Democratic and Republican Senatorial and Congressional Campaign Committees provide campaign funds, information about the legislative voting records of opponents and help with speech writing. In the 1980 elections the RNC and the Republican Senatorial and Congressional Campaign Committees worked closely to train and finance candidates fighting key targeted seats held by Democrats. The Republican Senatorial Campaign Committee gave $0.5 million on their behalf generally, while the Republican Congressional Campaign Committee contributed $1.8 million to House candidates and spent $0.8 million generally.

State party organisation
The fifty state committees vary greatly in terms of composition, selection procedures and numbers, but all have one thing in common – they are closely regulated by *state* law. Generally Republican state organisations tend to be stronger than the Democrats and provide more resources in terms of finance and campaign instruction and research. A recent survey of state committee chairmen revealed that they have little involvement in national committee affairs, while national party organisations' intervention in state matters reflected the ways in which the DNC and RNC have developed their roles, the RNC providing organisation and services while the DNC was more concerned with ensuring party rules over delegate selection were followed. Gener-

ally, however, both tend not to intervene with state party organisation, unless asked.

County committees

Historically, the 'county courthouse' is at the centre of state politics, as the county is the basic political division of the state. A considerable number of public officials are elected within the county and they control the political patronage of the area. Consequently the county committee is the most important part of the state party organisation. Delegates from county committees form the State General Committee of the party.

Ward and precinct committees

Grassroots political organisation in the parties means precinct politics. In the 178,000 precincts or voting districts, leaders are chosen by local party members. The method of election, either by primary or precinct caucus, varies from state to state and is determined by state law, which regulates all party activity. Precinct committees organise elections, recruit new members and generally maintain close contact with local voters. As at the local level in other countries, thousands of positions remain unfilled as it is often difficult to find people to perform the necessary routine tasks of political parties.

What of the future for American political parties? While there may be a hierarchical structure of party organisation, there is little control from the national committee of state and local parties, where the latter are left generally to administer their own affairs – to select candidates for political office, fund-raise, and run the state and county government if victorious.

At the national level, the rise of personal campaign organisations for presidential candidates, and increasingly for candidates in House and Senate elections, has meant that national party committees have fewer functions to perform. Traditional party functions, such as fund-raising, dispensing patronage, writing the party platforms and planning election strategy, have been largely taken over by these candidate-centred organisations.

However, national parties still have a role to perform and, in the aftermath of recent party reforms, it could be argued that they have been strengthened *vis-à-vis* state parties. But in American politics it is not necessarily party *organisation* that is important, but party *label*.

Political parties and elections

A political party may be defined as an organisation which sponsors canidates for political office under its name. Over one million offices, from the local school board to the presidency, are filled by election, and political parties contribute to the democratic nature of American politics through the functions they perform in the political system.

The traditional role of party and elections

Parties can be said to perform several roles in the political system:

(*a*) *They recruit candidates for office*, and provide campaign support in terms of policies, money and manpower to get them elected.

(*b*) *Parties formulate policy*. Parties develop proposals for the next election and criticise opposition policies.

(*c*) *Parties generate an interest in political matters*, drawing attention to issues and simplifying voters' choices by organising candidates into party tickets on the ballot paper.

(*d*) *Parties provide information to the electorate about politics*. They give cues to party supporters on issues of the day.

(*e*) *Parties channel demands of different groups and voters in society to elected officials*, and in so doing promote compromise among conflicting interests and encourage consensus in the political system.

However, in the last two decades the functions that parties perform has been challenged by new developments in the political systems.

The challenge to party in the political system

In recent years several important changes have occurred which have affected the roles that political parties play in the United States.

1. Development of the 'new politics'   This term originated with the campaign of Eugene McCarthy in 1968, where young political activists infiltrated into and attempted to capture the Democratic

Party nomination process and organise voters at grassroots level. Similarly, in 1972 George McGovern adopted a similar campaign strategy and was successful in winning the Democratic Party nomination for the presidency.

A second aspect of the 'new politics' is the use that candidates make of the mass media, opinion polls and public relations consultants. Firstly, candidates bypass political parties as channels of communication to the electorate and rely on political advertising and appeals through television and the press. Secondly, marketing methods and opinion polls are used systematically to identify voter concerns, and the candidate then focuses his attention on these issues.

The use of advanced technology, controlled by a professional campaign manager, has replaced the traditional method of party mobilisation of the electorate by door-to-door canvassing.

2. Rise of candidate-oriented organisations   Candidates for Congress and the presidency today depend less on party as a resource for workers, organisation and money. Party reforms of the nominating process (see below) encourage intra-party contests and, to challenge any incumbent, candidates have to develop their own organisation to capture their party's nomination. Vast amounts of cash were given to Richard Nixon's committee, CREEP, which orchestrated his 1972 presidential campaign, rather than to the Republican Party. Candidates also attract helpers for their campaigns on the basis of their stands on the political issues of the day, and so individuals become politically active because they are drawn to a particular candidate and not necessarily because they support the candidate's party. Hence those people who worked for Eugene McCarthy in 1968 provided a reservoir of support for George McGovern when he ran for the presidency in 1972.

In 1988, George Bush assembled a personal campaign organisation, headed by James Baker, whose influential members were leaders in Ronald Reagan's campaigns for the presidency in 1980 and 1984.

3. Changes in financing elections   Perhaps the most important change which has undermined political parties has been the 1974 Federal Election Campaign Act (FECA) which imposed tough new rules for the full reporting of campaign contributions and expenditures. Enacted in the aftermath of reveleations of illegal funding of Richard Nixon's CREEP, FECA established the Federal Election Commission (FEC) to enforce the provision of the Act and to administer the public financing of presidential campaigns. Although the Act was designed to clean up the financing of elections in the aftermath of the Watergate episode, it has also had the effect of weakening political parties.

(a) *Candidates and not parties are allocated money.* Candidates seeking *nomination* for President can qualify for federal funding by raising $5,000 (in individual contributions no greater than $250 each) in each of twenty states. The FEC matches these contributions up to half the spending limit, which in 1988 was $22 million per candidate. For the general election campaign, presidential candidates, provided they spend *only* public funds, receive twice the primary election limit. In 1988 this amounted to $44 million.

Parties are provided with public funds to finance their conventions and a small amount for general campaigning. The public funding of *candidates* as distinct from *parties* undermines parties as campaign managers as the removal of funds makes it difficult for them to finance and develop a campaign strategy.

(b) *Public funding creates personal campaign organisations.* To adhere to the strict contribution and disclosure provisions of FECA, candidates have had highly centralised and tightly controlled organisations. To gain maximum benefit from public funding, campaign planning needs to start earlier, direct mail solicitation for funds is more important and lawyers, accountants and computer specialists emerge as key people in the organisation.

(c) *Funding personalises election campaigns.* As federal funds are given to candidates, the consequence has been 'personalisation' of election campaigns. Candidates allocate most of their funding for television advertising which focuses on themselves and often blurs their party affiliation. Ronald Reagan's advertisement appealing to Democratic Party supporters, by identifying himself with past Democratic Presidents like Roosevelt and Kennedy, illustrate this point.

(d) *Candidate funding fragments parties.* As funding is provided to individual candidates, parties have been weakened, particularly in contests for the presidential nomination, by a large number of politicians seeking that position. In 1988 for example there were seven Democratic and six Republican contenders seeking their parties' nomination for the presidency. Public funding, too, encourages candidates to stay in the race for the nomination past the point where they can secure victory.

(e) *The proliferation of political action committees.* Following a Supreme Court decision in 1975, there has been a tremendous growth, from 722 to over 4,000 by 1988, in the number of political action committees (PACs) involved in electoral politics. Very quickly they surpassed party organisations in the money raised and spent in federal elections. Under federal law a PAC can give up to $5,000 for each separate election to each candidate. In 1984 the top ten PACs donated over $15 million to candidates seeking election. Political parties today provide candidates with only a small proportion of the finance needed to run an election and are virtually uninvolved in any other aspects of campaign fund-raising.

4. Party reform Since 1968 both parties, but particularly the Democrats, have adopted a series of reforms which were designed to encourage voter participation in the selection of their presidential nominees.

(a) *Reform of party rules.* Following the McGovern–Fraser Commission established in 1968, the Democratic Party established 18 'guidelines' for state parties to follow in selecting their delegates to the party's national convention. These rules, modified by the Mikulski Commission (1972–74) and the Winograd Commission (1975–78), have three main thrusts: (1) *to encourage participation* – all meetings selecting delegates to be well publicised and open to all party members; (2) *minority group representation* – women, young people and minority groups (blacks, Chicanos) should be represented in each state delegation to the national convention 'in reasonable relationship to their presence in the population of the state'; (3) *delegations to the national convention* should 'fairly reflect' the 'expressed presidential preference, uncommitted or no-preference status of the primary voters'. These reforms discouraged many long-time party regulars (the professionals), and made it easier for candidate and issue enthusiasts (the purists), who had little history of party service, to play significant roles at conventions and party meetings. The result was tension between party professionals who were concerned with winning elections, and the 'purists' who wished to maintain an ideological purity. The effects of these reforms had debilitating effects on both parties, but particularly the Democrats who introduced them. In 1988, in an attempt to balance 'purist' delegates at the convention, superdelegates were appointed drawn from both national and state politicians.

(b) *The proliferation of presidential primaries.* The un-planned consequences of rule changes has been the dramatic increase in the number of presidential primaries. In 1968 there were 17 primaries, by 1980 this number had risen to 37, and in 1988 to 38. Many state parties adopted the presidential primary as a method of selecting national convention delegates, this being the simplest way of conforming to the new rules laid down by the Democratic Party. These changes were often enshrined in state law, as the Democratic Party controlled many state governments, thus the Republicans had little option but to adopt the same procedures.

The effect of these rules changes and the proliferation of presidential primaries has been a trebling of the number of people involved in the selection of candidates for the presidency. In 1968 about 11 million people voted in the primaries, but by 1988 this number had risen to over 35 million. But more importantly, the rule changes challenge the assumption that American parties are decentralised and fragmented and that the national organisations have little power.

(a) *The new rules have led to centralisation.* Until the 1970s the state parties determined the composition of the delegation to the national convention. Today, the new rules lay down strict guidelines on the selection of delegates, and if these rules are breached by state delegations they will not be seated at the convention. State party organisations, fearing they will lose their seats, have complied. It was seen that the new rules have teeth when the 1972 Democratic Party Convention refused to seat the delegation from Cook County, Chicago, Illinois, led by Mayor Daley.

(*b*) *Legal supremacy of national party rules over state law*. Some of the Democratic Party rules conflict with the provisions of state statutes. The 1972 Democratic primary in Illinois was conducted under state law; this led to a court case, *Cousins* v. *Wigoda*, which in 1975 reached the Supreme Court, where it was decided that national party rules were in most circumstances superior to state laws.

In the 1980s the national party organisations have both the political and legal power to make the rules governing the presidential nominating process. But at the same time, changes in the rules have weakened the power of state and national party leaders in selecting a candidate for the presidency for the following reasons:

(*a*) *As we have seen, the new rules encourage greater participation in the selection of delegates*; consequently party leaders in the states and counties carry less weight.

(*b*) *The representation of minority groups has produced a higher proportion of young, women and black delegates*, again disadvantaging the old-style party regular who would support the party year in, year out, regardless of the party's candidate choice.

The internal reform of the Democratic and to a lesser extent the Republican parties, the reforms affecting the funding of elections and changes in campaign techniques, have together weakened the political parties. But can the parties adapt to the changing political environment?

Political parties: do they have a future?

Many political scientists have suggested that political parties are in trouble. They point out that:

(*a*) *Electorally parties are suffering a loss of support*. The turnout in the 1980 presidential election was 53.9 per cent and in 1984 and 1988 53 per cent. For congressional and state elections the figure is below 50 per cent.

(*b*) *The rise of candidate-centred politics* for the presidency, the Senate and, increasingly, contests for the House of Representatives, independent of party, have supplanted parties as election organisers.

(*c*) *Federal government reforms of election finance laws mean that parties are no longer the sole source of finance for candidates' election expenses.*

(*d*) *The media, and especially the way candidates use advertising*, means that parties have less control over the sources and type of information presented to the electorate about politics.

This evidence does suggest that parties have a bleak future. But there have always been attacks and criticisms of the American party system. Political parties are, arguably, in a permanent state of change and adaption, responding to new developments in the political environment.

Illustrations from recent elections suggest that political parties are meeting these new political challenges.

At the national level

1. The development of a national election strategy In 1980 Reagan's campaign emphasised the need for more Republicans in the House and Senate. In the so-called Republican Capitol Compact, the Republican leadership in Congress pledged their support to the five major policy goals of the Reagan campaign.

Similarly, in the 1982 mid-term elections, the Democratic Party leadership in Congress organised a national campaign for party candidates attacking the unfairness of the Reagan budget cuts and outling a programme for economic growth.

In 1986 President Reagan travelled 25,000 miles campaigning for Republican candidates, asking the electorate to vote for him 'one more time' – he did not want to be condemned to a six-year presidency with a Democrat-controlled Congress.

Recent research based on interviews with candidates for congressional elections suggest that national parties provide assistance in campaign management, campaign communications, fund-raising and gauging public opinion.

2. Parties are trying to recapture their role as fund-raisers. Election law allows the national parties to fund a state party's share of election expenses if the latter agrees to let the national organisation be its 'agent'. In this way the national Republican Senatorial Campaign Committee in 1980 doubled the amount it spent for some candidates, paying its and the state party's contributions.

Details of party financial activity over the last decade show that the DNC income has increased by $33 million between 1976 and 1984 while the Republicans grew by an impressive $75 million. Both parties, too, have developed a wide range of fund-raising programmes designed to solicit contributions from individuals and PACs. Typical of these programmes are the DNC's Labour and Business Councils and the RNC's PAC40 Club.

3. Both Democratic and Republican Parties are providing sophisticated training for candidates and campaign managers in campaign management and techniques. Both parties now provide candidates and state party organisations with a full range of campaign services. Minnesota State Republican chairman George McMath summed up the new attitude: 'We intend to provide services to candidates that will free them from reliance on professionals who are costly but can really give you nothing but advice.'

Both parties, too, are now located in their own offices and facilities are now provided for meetings, fund-raising functions, candidate briefings and political consultations. Permanent staff have also increased from 30 full-time DNC employees in 1972 to 130 in 1984 but the Republicans' staff rocketed from 30 to 600 in the same period. With the growth in staffs has come specialisation with each party establishing a political division to monitor the progress of candidates, a research division and a communications division which functions in an advertising agency producing television commericals during election years.

4. Parties realise that they are no longer the sole communicators of political information to the electorate and that they have to co-exist with the mass media They compete with interest groups and with the government for the voters' ear. But by acting in a co-ordinated manner, as did the Republicans in 1980 with their national television advertising campaign costing almost $10 million, they can present a party perspective and party information on the political issues of the day.

At the state and local level

1. Is party activism on the increase? Despite the emphasis on media campaigning, recent data suggests that local party activism is on the increase. Data from 1952 indicates that only 12 per cent of the public were contacted by campaign workers, by 1976 it was close to 30 per cent and in 1980 it was 24 per cent.

Local party contact has increased in all regions of the country and among all socio-economic groups. Today many more voters are being contacted by campaign workers. Does this suggest that party activism is on the decline?

2. Has there been a decline in public support and confidence in parties? Evidence from the 1970s suggest that voters are certainly less likely to evaluate candidates in 'party' terms, and are similarly less positive in their general evaluations of political parties. In 1960, 71 per cent of voters saw parties in a positive light, but by 1976 this figure had fallen to 49 per cent. Perhaps the most importance factor in the public's evaluation of parties is that today over 50 per cent of the electorate see neither party as capable of solving America's political and economic problems. Does this suggest that America is moving into a period of party realignment, with a less partisan and politically committed electorate awaiting mobilisation by realigned political parties?

Conclusion

Parties given the challenges to their traditional function of campaigning, fund-raising and representing public opinion in politics will not regain the prominent position they once had. Simply, there is too much competition from other sources. The puzzle that emerges in the 1980s is that parties are responding to the challenges presented to them. Neither party activism or party organisations are declining, *but* parties are seen as less relevant to offering solutions to America's problems.

That parties have survived in American politics for over two hundred years is evidence of their adaptability, and there is no reason to think that, even in a changed political environment, they will not continue to play a major role in political life.

Further reading

W. N. Chambers and W. D. Burnham (eds.), *The American Party Systems*, 2nd edn, Oxford University Press, 1975.
W. Crotty, *The Party Game*, Freeman, 1985.

S. J. Eldersveld, *Political Parties in American Society*, Basic
    Books, 1982.
X. Kayden and E. Mahe, *The Party Goes On*, Basic Books, 1986.

Questions

1. Does America have a two-party system?
2. Are political parties becoming obsolete?

8

INTEREST GROUPS

Introduction

In the United States, as with other democracies, other institutions exist apart from political parties to organise and transmit to government and politicians the views of particular sections of society. These organisations are called interest or pressure groups, and they provide a link between the people and their government. The distinction between political parties and interest groups is often hard to draw but, generally, political parties nominate candidates for elective office, seek to win and then staff those offices, and achieve this by appealing to the electorate in particularly defined constituencies. Interest groups, on the other hand, do not usually offer candidates for election or seek to exercise political power through office-holding, but attempt to affect public policy by influencing public opinion and, through mobilising public opinion, affect the decisions of the legislature. Interest groups will also appear as witnesses at congressional hearings, and provide evidence to government departments of the effect of public policy on their specific area of concern. An interest group may thus be defined as 'an organised body of individuals who share some goals and who try to influence public policy' (David Truman, *The Governmental Process*, Knox, 1951).

Often, however, the distinction between political parties and interest groups becomes blurred. Today many groups endorse candidates for office, provide campaign funds and workers, buy television advertising, and generally help at election time. For example, in the 1980 elections the broadly based interest group, Moral Majority, Inc., provided campaign funds and political support for selected conservative Republican candidates, while in 1988, the Liberty Federation, Moral Majority's successor, provided funds and television advertising for both George Bush and conservative Republican congressional candidates. However, some groups provide resources for both political parties, while others prefer to remain aloof from electoral conflict in order to appeal to both parties on an equal basis.

Interest groups should not be seen as rivals to political parties, for they complement each other, and in the complex nature of a modern democracy like the United States, with many access points in the political system, both institutions can coexist.

But the question remains, do interest groups pose a threat or contribute to the proper functioning of democracy in the United States? An early writer on American politics, Alexis de Tocqueville, wrote in *Democracy in America* (Oxford University Press, 1961) that Americans 'constantly form associations', suggesting that the political system was open and democratic. While on the other hand, James Madison in *The Federalist*, No. 10, warned of the dangers of 'faction' and reasoned that it would be inevitable that substantial differences would develop between such factions, and that each interest would do what it could to prevail over any other to persuade government to adopt policies it favoured. More recently President Eisenhower warned in his Farewell Address of the 'power of the military industrial complex' whose 'total influence – economic, political and even spiritual is felt in every city, every state house, every office of the federal government'.

These views, expressed almost two hundred years apart, indicate the ambivalence which many Americans feel about interest-group activity. Giving people the freedom to organise interest groups does not guarantee that society will end up with equally powerful pressure groups acting on their behalf. Inequalities exist in the interest-group system, with some sections of society, notably the wealthier, better-educated and business communities considerably better placed to organise then the poorer and less well educated. So do some people form pressure groups more easily than others, and are some interests represented while others are not?

How interest groups form

Each interest group has its own history and special circumstances surrounding its formation, but political scientists have suggested

three linked factors that are important in determining whether
interest groups develop or not.

*1. When a group of unorganised people are adversely affected by
change* David Truman, in *The Governmental Process*, suggested that interest groups form naturally when the need arises.
Hence when government attempts to regulate some social, political, or economic activity those individuals affected will come
together to lobby government not to take action which will affect
their well-being. For example, when President Reagan announced his rearmament programme and the manufacture of the
neutron bomb, the Nuclear Freeze Groups began a series of
protests attracting much public support against the President's
policies.

This idea of interest-group formation is similar to the 'invisible
hand' theory of classical economics, that self-correcting forces
will remedy an imbalance in the market-place, that there will be
an equilibrium among existing groups until some disturbance in
the political system forces new groups to form.

But does this view reflect the reality of political life? Change
alone does not ensure that a new interest group will form, while
some pressure groups have been formed in the absence of such
disturbances.

2. Interest-group leadership A factor which has been crucial in
determining the success of an interest group has been the quality
of its leadership. If an interest group is to be successful, its
leadership must be able to convince potential members that the
benefits they will receive from joining the group outweigh the
costs of membership. For example, Martin Luther King was able
to persuade many black Americans that the benefits of full
citizenship they would obtain after a long campaign for civil
rights outweighted the personal violence and deprivation that
many would suffer while achieving that goal. King's campaign of
passive resistance attracted much needed support from leading
white politicians and the passage of the Civil Rights Act in 1964
and the Voting Rights Act in 1965 were due in no small part to his
leadership of the black community.

3. Socio-economic structure of interest-group membership In
addition to group leadership perhaps a critical factor is the

'quality' of group membership. The well educated and better off
have more knowledge of how the political system operates and
more confidence that their activity can make a difference. These
factors give such people more incentive to devote time and
resources to organising and supporting interest groups. As
Martin Luther King and his Southern Christian Leadership
Conference illustrate, given charismatic leadership and a just
cause, the poor and politically inexperienced can achieve substantial political objectives.

Despite this example, there are inequalities in interest-group
representation and business and professional groups have an
inherent advantage because of their greater wealth and organisational abilities. The question then is not *by whom* but *how
well* are people represented.

Growth of interest groups

The last half-century has seen an increase in the number of
interest groups involved in politics. A recent survey of Wash-
ington-based lobbies revealed that some 30 per cent of current
interest groups were formed between 1960 and 1980. Two factors
seem to explain the growth of interest-group politics:

*1. The increase in the scope and power of government in
society* Following the New Deal era, governmental activity has
penetrated into every aspect of social, economic and political
life. Today the federal government has taken responsibility not
only for the defence of the nation, but also for managing the
economy and ensuring the welfare of its citizens. The enactment
of civil rights legislation, for example, has given the federal
government the positive responsibility for guaranteeing the
rights of black Americans in a majority white society. Similarly,
public concern over environmental pollution led to the creation
of the Environmental Protection Agency (EPA) which gives the
federal government further powers to regulate private business
interests.

*2. The decreasing power of individuals to secure their objectives
privately* As modern life has become more complex and
specialisation has increased, the power and capacity of the
individual to affect governmental outcomes has diminished.

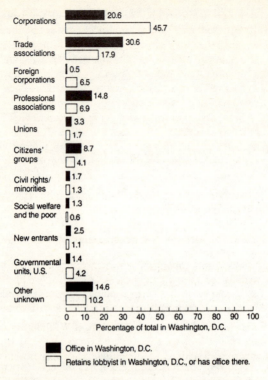

Corporations 20.6 / 45.7
Trade associations 30.6 / 17.9
Foreign corporations 0.5 / 6.5
Professional associations 14.8 / 6.9
Unions 3.3 / 1.7
Citizens' groups 8.7 / 4.1
Civil rights/minorities 1.7 / 1.3
Social welfare and the poor 1.3 / 0.6
New entrants 2.5 / 1.1
Governmental units, U.S. 1.4 / 4.2
Other unknown 14.6 / 10.2

0 10 20 30 40 50 60 70 80 90 100
Percentage of total in Washington, D.C.

■ Office in Washington, D.C.
☐ Retains lobbyist in Washington, D.C., or has office there.

Figure 8.1. Interest group representation in Washington

Hence, individuals who share common goals and aspirations have bonded together with groups to influence government and direct it to their concerns.

Interest groups tend then to proliferate both when society becomes more complex and specialised and when government activity expands in society.

Types of interest groups

The number and types of interest groups has grown sharply in recent years. More and more have found it useful to make their headquarters in Washington: by 1986 2,000 organisations with over 50,000 employees were located there.

The diversity of interest groups represented in Washington can be seen in Figure 8.1. As the figure illustrates, almost half of the interest-group representation in the capital are corporations or business trade associations, from which it might be argued that they have advantage over other groups represented.

Interest groups can be divided into five broad categories: economic interest groups, public interest groups, sectional groups, attitude groups and intergovernmental interest groups.

Economic interest groups

This category includes business and trade-union groups as well as individual companies which maintain full-time officers and staff in the capital.

1. Trade associations   The number of business and trade associations in Washington are more in evidence than ever before. A trade association, for example, the National Electrical Manufacturers Association, is an organisation that represents companies within the same industry. While the American equivalent of the Confederation of British Industry, the National Association of Manufacturers (NAM) represents over 14,000 companies, is highly conservative and in recent years has opposed legislation concerned with environmental protection.

The increase in business representation in Washington in the last twenty years is in part a response to the recent expansion of federal government activity. As new regulatory agencies, like the EPA, were created, many companies found themselves affected by new regulations and could only *react* to policies already made, and not participate in formulating those policies. Business groups saw the establishment of offices in the capital, essential if they were to influence the formation of government policy.

2. Giant private corporations   Many great industrial corporations, like General Motors and Boeing Aircraft Corporation, also have permanent representation in Washington. With large federal contracts often at stake, for example the Stealth bomber, each corporation must ensure that their interests are protected. The size and power of these individual companies rival that of government, and the political weight they carry is enormous. Business lobbies have a great advantage in that they are able to draw on the resources of their companies and they can fund their operations more easily than groups who depend on voluntary contributions.

3. Trade unions   The American equivalent to the British Trades Union Congress is the American Federation of Labor–Congress of Industrial Organisations (AFL–CIO). In 1984 the AFL–CIO had approximately 18 million members, about 20 per cent of the workforce. In recent years membership has been falling as the unionised industries in the North-East, for example steel and coalmining, decline. However, employment opportunities have increased in the tertiary sector of the company, based in the South and West, where unionisation has proved more difficult. The effectiveness of the AFL–CIO as a political force was well illustrated in 1959 when it failed to prevent the enactment of the Landrum–Griffin Act, which outlawed secondary picketing by trade-union members. The trade-union movement has been further weakened by allegations of widespread racketeering, disclosures of union corruption and infiltration by organised crime. Two presidents of the Teamsters Union (the transport workers' union), David Beck and Jimmy Hoffa, have been sent to jail. American unions, however, have been successful in advancing the living standards of their members mainly because they have concentrated their efforts on making bread-and-butter gains through collective bargaining. Because of individual union autonomy the AFL–CIO is a fairly weak national organisation.

4. Professional associations   Included in this category are such organisations as the American Bar Association (ABA) and the American Medical Association (AMA). The ABA plays an important role in the selection and nomination of judges in the American legal system and as an important source of advice and interpreter of legal questions in the political system.

The AMA, in particular, has always been deeply involved in politics. In the 1960s it fought unsuccessfully the introduction of Medicare (federal health insurance) and Medicaid (medical aid for the poor). By the 1980s it was one of the largest spending interest groups at election time, providing over $2 million for federal candidates who were supportive of its conservative political stance.

Public-interest groups

In recent years, following increased public concern with such issues as consumer protection and environmental pollution, new groups have emerged as an articulate voice of the *public*, as distinct from the *private* interest. The growth in public-interest groups can be explained partly by change in the early 1970s of American attitudes towards government. At this time, following US intervention in Vietnam, the failure of the Great Society programmes and Watergate, Americans became more cynical about government and its ability to solve many of the problems facing the nation. As a consequence, people turned to interest groups who spoke out on and appeared effective in dealing with single issues, such as consumer protection and the environment. Prominent among these groups are:

1. Common Cause This organisation was founded by John Gardner, former Secretary of the Department of Health Education and Welfare in the Johnson administration. The best known of the 'good government' groups, Common Cause achieved success fighting in the courts to clean up the financing of federal election campaigns, ethics codes in government and open congressional and administrative proceedings.

2. The Nader organisations Perhaps the best-known public interest activist, Ralph Nader first came to public attention in 1966 when he exposed the unroadworthiness of the Corvair motor car. His success, following General Motors' withdrawal of this vehicle, led Nader to join with others to form a series of public interest groups. For example, Congress Watch concentrates on consumer affairs, the environment, transportation and congressional reform, while the Center for Auto Safety continues Nader's pioneering work in the field of road safety. Nader's reputation as a relentless driven lobbyist for consumer protection, where opponents are treated as 'enemies of the people', has made his organisation a highly effective campaigner in Washington.

The distinction between such public interest groups as Common Cause and the Nader organisation is that they represent the *consumer interest* as against the *producer interests* in society where the latter have so dominated interest group activity.

Sectional groups
These work to defend and promote the interests of specific social groups in American society. In recent years the struggle for

equal rights by black Americans and women have been brought
to prominence by interest groups working in these areas.

*1. National Association for the Advancement of Colored People
(NAACP)* Founded in 1909, the NAACP stressed that legal
action in the courts and lobbying in Congress for civil rights
legislation was the way to achieve equal rights for black Americans. In 1954 NAACP sponsored a series of school desegrega-
tion cases including *Brown* v. *Board of Education of Topeka,
Kansas* (see Chapter 4). To many black Americans in the 1950s,
the gradualism of the NAACP was unacceptable and demands
began to be heard for 'freedom now'. Against this background
Dr Martin Luther King founded the Southern Christian Leadership Conference to advanced black rights through non-violent,
direct action.

The culmination of the struggles of both black pressure
groups came in the 1960s and 1970s with congressional legislation designed to outlaw racial discrimination.

2. Women's rights Although Equal Rights Amendments have
been debated in Congress since 1923, the 1970s saw an increase
in the strength of the women's movement. Two organisations,
the National Women's Political Caucus and the National Organization for Women (NOW), have campaigned extensively for
women's rights, particularly in the areas of abortion law reform,
the rights of lesbians and the ratification of the Equal Rights
Amendment by the states.

Attitude groups
Perhaps the fastest growing and most powerful political organisations in the United States, these groups share common
beliefs and objectives on one particular issue and perceive their
major roles, apart from lobbying before Congress, as mobilising
support, both financial and electoral, in the country for candidates for political office who share their views.

Currently the most prominent of these new attitude groups,
most of which represent the 'New Right', is the fundamentalist
Christian group led by Jerry Falwell, Moral Majority, Inc. (now
a part of the founder's new organisation Liberty Federation).
Along with other groups such as Phyllis Schlafy's Eagle Forum
and the Conservative Coalition, Moral Majority advocates
policies they consider in line with biblical teachings (such as

prayers in school), are against the teaching of the Darwinian theory of evolution and want to restrict abortion.

These groups have been very successful in raising funds for political purposes through appeals in weekly televised religious gatherings. In the 1980 elections, these powerful organisations embarked on a crusade against certain liberal Democrats, particularly Senators Birch Bayh, George McGovern and Frank Church, and were instrumental in bringing about their defeat. In recent elections, however, their success rate in defeating alleged 'liberal' members of Congress has declined dramatically.

But during the Reagan presidency, these conservative citizen groups have enjoyed substantial access to the White House, but they cannot claim the same degree of success with Congress, where such goals as a constitutional amendment allowing school prayer remain unfulfilled. Nevertheless, continued Republican presidential victories have given these groups and their conservative political values political visibility in the 1980s.

Intergovernmental interest groups
The growth in federal government programmes in the last couple of decades, particularly in the area of urban renewal, poverty, and consumer protection has led to an expanded role being played by state and city governments as administrative agents for the central government. This has led naturally to a greater interdependence between sub-national (state and city) and national governments and given rise to what has become known as the 'intergovernmental lobby'. Today in Washington, state governments and individual cities frequently have their own offices, in addition to such umbrella organisations as the National Governors' Conference, US Conference of Mayors and the National Association of Counties.

The immense growth of interest groups, particularly in the area of consumer and governmental protection and the intergovernmental lobby, is one of the legacies of the recent reform period in American politics. New groups with an interest in new programmes are drawn to Washington as the centre of political action to press their claims on the federal government.

Interest group tactics in Washington
In the American system, interest groups have three main access points where they can try to influence governmental decisions:

the Congress; bureaucrats and officials within the executive branch; and, to a limited extent, the judiciary.

Interest groups and Congress

1. Interest groups appear as witnesses at the investigative hearings held by committees of Congress Usually they prepare testimony beforehand and answer questions put by committee members. Interest groups will often discuss strategy with a friendly member of the committee who might offer advice on tactics and lines of approach.

2. Interest groups attempt personal contact with Congressmen usually in the legislator's office or in a more informal environment – over drinks, for example. With the growth in Congressmen's personal staff, and the increased reliance that legislators place on them, interest groups try to develop contacts with personal aides. Groups are aware that staff members offer advice to Congressmen, and consequently quiet cultivation can bring long-term benefits.

A variation of the indirect approach is that interest groups will 'lobby' one Congressmen to approach another on their behalf. Also, groups will arrange meetings between bureaucrats and important constituency members sympathetic to their cause, to influence a legislator.

3. Interest groups and public opinion Groups attempt to mould public opinion through the use of the press, television and radio. To influence Congressmen in particular, interest groups often organise letter-writing campaigns from constituents back home in an attempt to show how widespread local feelings are on a particular issue. However, an avalanche of mail, particularly if all the letters read alike, often fails to impress and is usually discounted. On the other hand, a few letters from opinion-leaders in a Congressman's district, for example from a campaign contributor, or a powerful union official, often carry more weight.

In general, although important interest groups like the AMA do use these opinion-moulding techniques, there is no guarantee of success; for although vast sums of money may be spent, legislation to which powerful groups are opposed is often enacted. For instance, as noted above, Medicare and Medicaid were introduced in spite of well-publicised and expensive media campaigns.

A final tactic which an interest group may resort to if conventional lobbying seems unsuccessful is political protest. Such activities, a march or demonstration, are designed to attract media attention, and protestors hope that television and newspaper coverage will make politicians more receptive to their group's views. The Freeze Movement's 'Hands across America' to protest against President Reagan's nuclear rearmament programme is an example of this type of event. The main disadvantage of this type of protest is that policy making is a long-term incremental process while demonstrations are short lived. It is often difficult to sustain the enthusiasm of group members in protest after protest in order to keep a group's views in the public eye. Perhaps an exception to this were the long-term civil rights campaigns in the 1950s and 1960s, involving protest marches and lunch counter sit-ins. Certainly American public opinion was influenced in favour of the protesters after seeing the police use of dogs and high-powered hoses against peaceful black demonstrations in Alabama, and the change in public opinion hastened the passage of civil rights legislation in the 1960s.

4. Interest groups and the growth of political action committees In recent years many interest groups have created PACs to raise money from members and donate those funds to finance the election campaigns of selected politicians. Following a change in the law prohibiting corporations forming PACs in 1974, each PAC can give up to $5,000 for each separate election to a candidate for Congress.

Figure 8.2 illustrates the growth in PACs particularly since 1974, and by the end of 1988 over 4,000 were registered with the FEC. Interest groups form PACs because they believe that campaign contributions help when they are trying to gain access to Congressmen. A Congressman will find it very difficult to refuse a meeting with a lobbyist who made a campaign contribution at the last election.

Interest groups are also very pragmatic when it comes to making campaign contributions. In the 1988 elections, corporate PACs gave 80 per cent of their contributions to incumbent

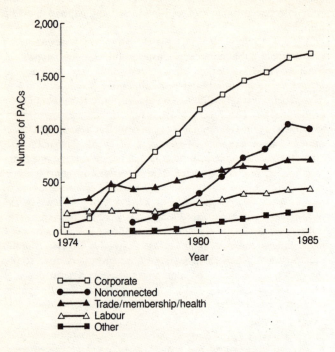

Figure 8.2. Growth of political action committees

members of Congress, many of them liberal or moderate Democrats. As one commentator has noted, access to those in powerful positions, such as committee chair, is more important than supporting ideological friends.

The provision of funds does not imply that PACs buy the loyalty of candidates seeking election, but any legislator must feel indebted to his financial backers, especially when their interests are at stake in some public decision.

The activities of interest groups in the legislature are regulated by Act of Congress, although minimally. A 1909 statute makes it illegal to offer a bribe to a member of Congress, while the 1946 Federal Regulation of Lobbying Act requires individuals and organisations who are engaged 'principally' in paid lobbying

activities to register and file reports on money spent to 'aid ...
the passage or defeat of any legislation by Congress'. However,
many groups do not register because they argue that lobbying is
not their 'principal' function and thus the 1946 Act does not
effectively regulate interest group activity in the legislature.

Although in 1978 several Democratic Congressmen were
accused of corruption in the 'Abscam' investigation, there is little
evidence of bribery evident in Congress today. However, many
interest groups provide lavish hospitality for legislators – can this
be considered corruption?

Interest groups and the bureaucracy

Because many day-to-day decisions on policy are made within the
bureaucracy by departments of state and regulatory commissions,
interest groups are concerned that their views are represented in
the executive branch. Bureaucrats in their turn welcome interest
groups as a source of information and support, both in conflicts
with other agencies within the executive branch and with Congress.

To have influence within the bureaucracy, interest groups have
adopted a number of approaches.

(a) *Interest groups seek to influence political appointments*.
For example, President Reagan's choice of Secretary of the
Interior, James Watt, was supported enthusiastically by gas, oil
and mineral interests anxious to see federally owned land made
available for exploitation.

(b) *Interest groups seek to become part of the bureaucrats'
decision-making process*. Bureaucrats need information on
how programmes are working, so where better to turn than to
those groups that are affected? For example, neighbourhood
associations were asked for ideas to organise and implement
the capital's urban and housing programmes.

(c) *Interest groups and policy initiatives*. Ideas for changes
in policy are usually generated by working groups within the
bureaucracy. Interest groups will attempt to gain access to
policy planning groups in order to help shape future proposals.

(d) *Officials and interest groups*. Expert interest-group
officials will maintain close personal contacts with key government officials to trade information and become a part of a
wider reference group that is consulted on policy.

(e) *Interest groups often support programmes in which they do not have a direct interest*. This is done to accrue credit that can be drawn upon later, when bureaucratic support may be needed for a programme that is central to a group's interest.

Arguably, a close relationship with the bureaucracy is the most important dimension of an interest group's work. Here they have a chance to shape new proposals and achieve incremental changes in existing policies through minor amendments to regulations.

Interest groups and the judiciary

In the United States the courts are a part of the political process, and judges make decisions concerning aspects of political, social and economic life which would in other countries be the responsibility of elected officials. The ethics of the judicial process, however, prevent the use of many of the techniques used by interest groups in the legislative and executive branches of government. Such tactics would not be tolerated by judges, and consequently interest groups have adopted approaches more suitable to the courtroom.

(*a*) *Influencing the selection of justices*. This is particularly important for the Supreme Court and the Federal Courts of Appeal. The most important group in the selection process is the ABA which often vets candidates for the federal court system. In recent years, interest groups have objected to particular nominations, for example, the NAACP and other civil rights groups lobbied successfully in the Senate to defeat the nomination of Harold Carswell and Clement Haynesworth, and more recently Robert Bork.

(*b*) *Sponsorship of test cases*. Interest groups have used litigation in the courts to make public policy in the absence of legislative action. The basic strategy of the NAACP was to use the courts, where it had relatively equal access with other groups in society. The NAACP provides litigants with legal services to fight cases and for example sponsored the *Brown* case in 1954 (see p. 114).

(*c*) *Public relations*. Interest groups often try to influence the climate of opinion in the judicial community. Lawyers sympathetic to certain interest groups' causes will seek to publish articles in the law journals read by judges. Again, the NAACP in its campaign against racial covenants in housing sought to influence legal opinion by persuading sociologists sympathetic to its view of the issue to publish in law journals.

The tactics of interest groups to influence the judiciary are of necessity more limited. Brash advertising campaigns and direct approaches to justices would be counter-productive. However, groups have tried to influence the climate of opinion in legal circles and have placed new issues on the political agenda through litigation.

Who rules America?

Interest groups appear to be weighted in favour of the more affluent, better-educated and well-organised sections of society; represent the private as against the public interest; and challenge the notion that the US political system is open and democratic. This raises questions about how the phrase 'government by the people' has been interpreted.

The majoritarian model of democracy

This is based on the classical theory of democracy where government by the people means government by the *majority* of the people. The basic idea underlying the majoritarian model is that of representative government, electing officials to make political decisions on behalf of society. Through the ballot box the public express their political preferences by choosing between alternative political parties or candidates, and control poltiticians by the threat of defeat at a future election. Supporters of the majoritarian view see elections as not only choosing candidates for office, but also deciding on governmental policies. People are not only expected to vote but are assumed to have a high degree of knowledge about politics and vote rationally for candidates that support their policy preferences.

Recent evidence suggests, however, that only a quarter of the electorate claim they 'followed what was going on' in government 'most of the time' while only 37 per cent said they followed politics 'now and then' or 'hardly at all'. Further, voter turnout in presidential elections in the 1980s is only a little over 50 per cent. It seems that the assumptions underlying the majoritarian model, and people's knowledge of and participation in politics, must therefore be questioned.

Pluralist model of democracy

The pluralist model recognises that individuals in society share common ethnic, religious or economic interests, and band together to form interest groups who then seek to influence government policy. The basis of the pluralist model is the *group* and not the *individual*, and that government by the people means government by the people *operating through interest groups*. The criterion for democracy is changed from elected officials and government responding to public opinion expressed through the ballot box, to the responsiveness to people organised into interest groups.

The pluralist model makes several assumptions about political society.

(*a*) *That government is decentralised and has many access points*. With a federal system, with both national and state governments, this is true. Further, at each level, national and state constitutions divide political authority between the executive, legislative and judicial branches of government.

(*b*) *That the political system is open to all*. That if there is an unrepresented interest in society it will not be prevented from organising and will have an opportunity to be heard. Thus public policy will be decided when the competing claims of various interest groups have been made.

Robert Dahl in his book *Who Governs?* (Yale University Press, 1961) is the foremost advocate of the pluralist model of democracy. He examined a series of controversial public issues in New Haven, Connecticut, and traced how decisions were made. Dahl concluded that although an elite existed in the town, the city's 'notables' did not run New Haven; instead some individuals and groups were influential in one issue area while a second group were more influential in another. Thus in different areas of policy, different individuals and groups dominated. To the pluralist, public policy evolves following conflict between competing interest groups which take place in an open political system.

The power elitists' view of democracy

The power elitists challenge the pluralist notion of democracy and argue that America is governed by a 'power elite', a 'power structure' or 'establishment'. In his book, *The Power Elite*, C. Wright Mills (Oxford University Press, 1956) suggests that a small group – 'the possessors of power, wealth, and celebrity' – occupies key positions in society – for instance, its members control what has become known as the military–industrial complex. This elite derives its power from the positions its members hold in society as the leaders of the great corporations and heads of the military machine; they work in a co-ordinated manner and govern the nation in their interest and not in the interests of the majority of the American people.

The neo-elitists' view of democracy

This group have criticised both the pluralists and the elitist conception of power, and argue that the wielders of power cannot always be identified by examining how decisions are made in society. They suggest that the truly powerful can exercise their authority to prevent certain political issues ever reaching the arena of public debate through the 'mobilisation of bias'. That is, interest groups will use the basic values of American society to stop issues being discussed. For example, the AMA were successful for many years in preventing the adoption of Medicare by suggesting that a 'socialised' national health system was the first step down the road to the United States becoming a communist state.

Despite the arguments of the supporters of majoritarianism and power elitists, there is general acceptance that the United States is a pluralist society and that there are many groups that have access to the government and that they compete with each other to influence public policy. On closer examination, perhaps, American pluralism is *really* competition between competing elites; interest groups are dominated by individuals from the politically motivated middle classes; while disadvantaged sections of society have neither the knowledge nor the money to organise their interests effectively. As Republican Senator Bob Dole has commented, 'there aren't any poor PACs or Food Stamp PACs or Nutrition PACs or Medicare PACs'.

Further reading

J. M. Berry, *The Interest Group Society*, Little, Brown, 1984.
N. Polsby, *Community Power and Political Theory*, 2nd edn, Yale University Press, 1980.
L. J. Sabato, *PAC Power*, Norton, 1984.
G. K. Wilson, *Interest Groups in the United States*, Clarendon Press, 1981.

Questions

1. Is interest group democracy democratic?
2. How effective are interest groups in influencing the government?

9

THE FEDERAL BUREAUCRACY

Introduction

In his inaaugural address in 1980, Ronald Reagan voiced the feelings of many Americans when he spoke of the need to get the government 'off the backs of the American people' and that one of his major priorities would be to 'curb the size and influence of the Federal Establishment': an establishment which had grown from three departments (State, Treasury and War), employing a few hundred people in 1789, to thirteen departments in 1980, with a civilian workforce of about 3 million people.

As the size of the federal government has grown, so too has the federal budget. President Kennedy in 1963 tried to keep his budget below $100 thousand million but President Reagan's last budget for fiscal year 1990 reached almost $1,200 thousand million. The increased size of the budget and the growth in the number of departments and administrative agencies can be explained by the growth of government intervention ·in many areas of social and economic life. The 1950s and 1960s saw government initiatives in the fields of civil rights, public housing, income maintenance, transportation and urban affairs, while the 1970s witnessed the rise of different and newer concerns: consumer protection, the preservation of the environment and energy conservation. Even in the 1980s, despite the Reagan rhetoric to reduce the size and scope of the federal government, interventionism continues and the federal budget increases.

The growth of the federal government

Although the size of the federal budget has doubled in real terms since 1960 and the number of agencies administering new programmes has increased, the overall size of the federal establishment has remained relatively stable. However, at the state and local level, the civilian workforce has increased from about 4.25 million in 1950 to 13 million in 1983. There are a number of reasons why the size of the government has grown.

1. Economic interventionism   The Great Crash in 1929 which triggered the Depression in the 1930s brought about a change in philosophical attitudes toward government intervention in the economy. In the nineteenth century a *laissez-faire* philosophy prevailed and economic regulation by government was seen as inappropriate. Although government had begun to regulate business practices in the late nineteenth and early twentieth centuries, the advent of Keynsian demand management economics in the 1930s led to the federal government taking responsibility for ensuring full employment and maintaining economic growth. These new responsibilities necessitated new bureaucratic agencies, for example the Securities Exchange Commission, through which the government became a referee in the economic market-place, developing standards of fair trade, setting rates and licensing businesses for operation. In the 1960s and 70s as new problem areas emerged, the federal government added new agencies, thereby expanding the range of activities.

2. Social welfare   Since the New Deal, attitudes towards the government's responsibilities to social welfare have changed. Prior to the 1930s the political culture placed great emphasis on self-reliance and people were expected to succeed on the basis of their own efforts. But following the Depression the federal government began to take responsibility for social welfare provision following the enactment of the Social Security Act 1935 which created Aid to Families with Dependent Children (AFDC). By 1983 roughly 11 million people each month were receiving benefits under this programme, costing $13.8 billion a year. President Johnson's Great Society legislation in 1965 extended social welfare benefits by enacting Medicare and Medicaid.

3. Complexity of society   Government has expanded as society has become more complex. As new issues have emerged, control of pollution and the environment, or space exploration for example, the federal government has been the only institution to cope with such matters which have a national remit. Thus new governmental agencies, the EPA and the National Aeronautics and Space Administration (NASA), are added to the federal government.

4. Natural bureaucratic expansion Once created, government bureaucracies have a tendency to expand to take on new responsibilities. Administrators look for new ways to serve their clients, new programmes are developed to meet changing needs, which in turn necessitate larger staffs and larger budgets.

The structure of the bureaucracy

The federal bureaucracy consists of four basic types of agencies: cabinet departments, independent regulatory commissions, independent executive agencies and government corporations.

Cabinet departments – or the Departments of State

The President's Cabinet is composed of the heads (Secretaries of State) of the thirteen executive departments, and these form the centre of the federal government administration. The increase in the number of departments has paralleled the growth of the American nation. The current departments, as at March 1989, are:

Date established	Department
1789	State
1789	Treasury
1849	Interior
1870	Justice
1889	Agriculture
1913	Commerce
1913	Labor
1949	Defense (amalgamation of War, Army, Navy and Airforce)
1953	Health, Education and Welfare
(1979	Health and Human Services)
1965	Housing and Urban Development
1966	Transportation
1978	Energy
1979	Education

The departments created in 1789 were the State Department, the Department of the Treasury, and the Department of War; although George Washington included the Attorney-General in his Cabinet, the Department of Justice was not established until 1870. The nineteenth century witnessed the gradual increase in the number of departments, two (Interior and Agriculture) reflecting dominant concerns of the age. But the last eighty years have seen the addition, excluding the Department of Defense, of a further seven departments, which reflects the colossal expansion of federal government activity in the economic and social life of the nation. The Department of Commerce and Labor was set up in 1903 (and divided in 1913), but the major growth came in the wake of Roosevelt's New Deal which created many new agencies to deal with the problems of unemployment and social welfare. In 1953 some of these amalgamated to form the Department of Health, Education and Welfare. Concerns with the problems of urban regeneration led Congress to establish the Department of Housing and Urban Development in 1965, and then in the following year the Department of Transportation was set up. In the 1970s America, in the aftermath of the Arab oil price rises, became concerned about its self-sufficiency as an energy producer and as a consequence the Department of Energy was established in 1978. Finally, just before President Carter's election defeat the Health, Education and Welfare Department was divided into the Departments of Education, and Health and Human Services.

Generally, the creation of Cabinet departments has been the culmination of a long process of the amalgamation of small agencies which were established to deal with specific problem areas: for example, the Bureau of Labor was formed in 1883 as part of the Department of the Interior, and achieved full department status in 1913.

Each Cabinet department is organised in a hierarchical pattern. The Secretary of State is at the top, and ranked below him are under-secretaries, deputy under-secretaries and assistant secretaries of state, all appointed by the President and confirmed by the Senate. The increase in federal government activity is reflected in the growth of political appointees in each department. For example, in 1933 the Department of Labor had a Secretary and two assistant secretaries of State, but by 1984, three deputy under-secretaries and six assistant secretaries were added as third- and fourth-tier political appointments.

Below these political appointees are the bureau chiefs, representing the senior level of career federal civil servants. Although there may seem to be a straightforward chain of command from the President downwards, Presidents often find it difficult, without spending a great deal of time and effort, to gain compliance from their subordinates. Similarly, it would be a mistake to see departments as monolithic structures. Bureaux within each department compete for financial and political resources to maintain their status and programmes. Congress has often reinforced this competition and consequent departmental fragmentation by allocating specific authority and funds to a particular bureau, leaving little discretion for the Secretary of State to develop an overall strategy for his department. Perhaps the best example of bureau independence within a Department of State is the position of the FBI in the Justice Department. Bureau chiefs, too, add to departmental fragmentation by cultivating influential Congressmen and Senators to gain political advantage over their superiors.

Independent regulatory commissions

The regulatory commissions occupy a special status in the federal bureaucracy. Commissions are established by an Act of Congress to perform a wide range of regulatory functions in many areas of industrial and commercial life. For example:

(a) *The Interstate Commerce Commission* (1887) regulates and fixes fares for railways, buses and freight companies.

(b) *The Federal Trade Commission* (1914) regulates industry and is responsible for preventing unfair competition, price-fixing and misleading advertising and other abuses.

(c) *The Federal Communications Commission* (1934) grants licences to television and radio stations.

(d) *The Securities and Exchange Commission* (1934) registers stockbrokers and regulates stock exchange and protects the public from investing in securities on the basis of false and misleading claims.

Each regulatory commission is headed by a board, whose members are appointed by the President for a fixed term of office. Consequently, a new President is often faced by an agency staffed by members he cannot dismiss, and it may be some time before he can make his own appointments. Furthermore, the power of appointment is circumscribed by statutory obligations which require members of boards to be drawn from both political parties.

The increase in the number of regulatory commissions can be explained by a number of factors:

(*a*) *Congress wished to control the expansion of presidential authority* over the bureaucracy.

(*b*) *The commissions are a response to the demand for government regulation* in many spheres of economic life.

(*c*) *Commissions are designed to take administration out of politics*. They are not specifically 'executive' agencies but are required to make rules and decide whether these rules have been broken. Regulatory commissions thus exercise quasi-legislative and quasi-judicial powers.

However, there has been severe criticism of the regulatory commissions. In practice it has been difficult to insulate their regulatory activities from politics. Presidents have attempted to influence board members, despite their fixed terms of appointment. Congress has used its legislative power to gain compliance. But more seriously, it has been suggested that the regulatory commissions have become *servants* of industry instead of regulating it in the public interest.

Independent executive agencies

Within the executive branch, there are about sixty independent agencies which are not part of any Cabinet department and are controlled in varying degrees by the President. Perhaps the most important of these is the CIA, headed by a Director who is directly under the President's control. Other agencies include the Veterans Administration and NASA.

Government corporations

The United States has avoided a policy of nationalisation of industry, but Congress, where it has decided that the public can be better served, has involved the federal government in such commercial and industrial enterprises as the Tennessee Valley Authority and, more recently, the Amtrak railway line.

Although these government corporations have some autonomy, they have been increasingly subject to executive and legislative control, particularly in their financial management.

The Federal Civil Service

A majority of posts in the civil service are filled by competition. However, a substantial number of posts are at the disposal of the President. A recent estimate has placed the figure at around 20,000 jobs, of which approximately 2,000 are senior political appointments. These include not only the obvious Cabinet and sub-Cabinet appointments, members of the Boards of the regulatory commissions, but a large number of positions as policy advisers to heads of agencies, which are, arguably, politically sensitive posts. The crucial point to observe in the American system is that political appointments are made well down into the civil service and are not just a thin layer on the top of the professional hierarchy.

This history of political appointees can be traced to the founding of the nation. Presidents have always rewarded their supporters with government jobs. Jefferson, when he became President, substituted Federalist Party supporters with Demo-cratic-Republicans; but the 'spoils system', as it became known, was institutionalised by Andrew Jackson when he replaced about 20 per cent of the Federal Service with his own supporters.

In the post-Civil War period, corruption and inefficiency led to demands for civil service reform, and in 1871 Congress estab-lished the first Civil Service Commission. Although this failed because of lack of funds, continued pressure for reform led to the Civil Service Act of 1883 (The Pendleton Act), which laid the foundation of the present Federal Service. The Act established a Civil Service Commission (now the Office of Personnel Manage-ment) which recruits staff on the basis of competitive examin-ations, operates a merit system of promotion and gives a degree of security of tenure to federal employees. Today, approximately 85 per cent of the civil service is recruited in this way.

In the United States, unlike some other countries, the civil service has a unified structure, with a number of salary grades ranging from GS (General Schedule) Grade 1 to Grade 18, within which appointments are made.

The Civil Service Acts have in effect created a dichotomy between career and non-career administrators, i.e., between political and non-political appointments. The Acts offer security of tenure to those in the bureaucracy who perform the ordinary tasks of administration in a totally non-political manner; thus there is deemed to be a separation between policy making which political appointees engage in, and administration, which career civil servants undertake. Recently, many Presidents, particularly Republicans, have felt that such a distinction is unreal, for even basic administrative actions generate political consequences. Republicans often claim that they find difficulty in controlling the civil service because many of its senior career officers were appointed by Democratic Presidents. This has led to demands by many Republicans for more political appointees at the top of the civil service hierarchy so that greater 'political control can be exercised'. But is an increase in the number of political appointees the way to control the bureaucracy, or should other and more sophisticated methods be adopted?

Control of the bureaucracy

The Constitution divides responsibility for the federal bureaucracy between the President and Congress.

The President and the bureaucracy

There are four ways that the President can attempt to control the bureaucracy.

(*a*) *Power of appointment*. The President appoints individuals to the Cabinet and sub-Cabinet positions in the departments as well as members of the Boards of Regulatory Commissions. The Senate has to confirm these appointments, and so acts as a check on presidential control. In recent years the Senate has refused several presidential nominations, for example Ernest W. Lefever, Ronald Reagan's choice as Assistant Secretary of State with special responsibility for human rights, and in 1989 refused to confirm President Bush's nominee, John Tower, as Secretary of State for Defense.

However, the power of appointment does not guarantee compliance on the part of the bureaucracy. Senior career civil servants are themselves experienced in bureaucratic politics; they control the flow of information to political appointees and can consequently influence any decisions that are taken. Political appointees may only be in a department for a few years and are faced with career civil servants with a lifetime of knowledge of their departments. The degree to which political appointees are co-opted by their departments was noted by John Ehrlichman, a prominent member of Nixon's White House staff, who commented 'We only see them at the annual White House Christmas Party: they go off and marry the natives.'

(b) *Reorganisation of the bureaucratic structure.* Often Presidents try to gain tighter control of the bureaucracy through administrative reform. Under the 1949 Reorganization Act, Congress gave Presidents the power to propose administrative reforms in the departments and regulatory commissions. Following directly from this, the Department of Health, Education and Welfare was created in 1953.

Richard Nixon attempted far-reaching reform in his 1971 Reorganization Bill. He proposed to transform seven Cabinet departments concerned principally with domestic politics into four 'super-departments' of Natural Resources, Community Development, Human Resources and Economic Affairs. Nixon's goal was tighter management of the bureaucracy over which his political appointees could exercise greater control. Congress, however, vetoed Nixon's proposals, as they saw them as a threat to their own control of the bureaucracy.

Reorganisation, too, lets the government respond to new political priorities. The creation of the Department of Energy by President Carter, in the wake of the Arab oil embargo of 1973 brought different agencies concerned with energy problems into one large unit to develop a co-ordinated policy to make the United States less dependent on foreign oil supplies.

(c) *The politicisation of the bureaucracy.* Presidents have attempted to extend political control of the bureaucracy by declassifying posts which are regarded as civil service appointments. For example, President Eisenhower in 1952 transformed a number of key posts into semi-political appointments which had hitherto been occupied by career civil servants appointments under a Democratic administration.

(d) *Budgetary control.* This is perhaps the most important and effective control of the bureaucracy. Through the OMB created in 1970, Presidents attempt fiscal management of the bureaucracy. Each spring, organisational departments submit plans for the future budgetary year. The OMB matches these requests against economic forecasts, and against this background the President establishes his budget guidelines. The competition among agencies for a slice of the budget cake gives the President, through OMB, a powerful level of bureaucratic control.

Congress and the bureaucracy

Congressional control of the bureaucracy is almost a mirror image of presidential control.

(a) *Presidential nominations have to be confirmed by the Senate.*

(b) *Congress has to approve presidential proposals to organise the the bureaucracy.* In the case of the Nixon Reorganization Plan of 1971, Congress chose not to implement the President's proposals as they would have necessitated a complete restructuring of the committee system. This would have upset the seniority system by which members of the House and Senate are allocated to committees (see Glossary).

(c) *Budgetary control and congressional oversight.* Congress scrutinises the presidential budget and has the constitutional authority to provide funds for the departments. Through hearings, the various congressional committee will probe and investigate the workings of each government department, scrutinising estimates and looking for maladministration. These committees have the power to call federal civil servants to give evidence and for close questioning.

The question is, how effective are the presidential and congressional controls on the bureaucracy? The federal bureaucracy has its own sources of power. The basis of that power is the ability of the civil service to build political support both within Congress and the executive branch. In recent years many agency heads have had close relationships with influential committee chairmen. For example, the military services have often been able to count on the support of the chairman of the Senate Armed Services Committee, Sam Nunn. Further evidence of the cultivation of Congressment by Departments of State can be seen in the number of civil servants who are engaged in liaison work. Today, about 700 individuals watch over legislation concerning their departments and generally help Congressmen with information and advice on current problems.

Bureaucrats also lobby on behalf of their agencies within the executive branch. They seek both political support and money for their projects from political appointees, who are often asked to adjudicate between competing bureaux within the same department.

Agencies also seek support outside the presidency and Congress. They seek support from the special interest groups with which they deal. The Agriculture Department works closely with farming interests, the Pentagon (the Defense Department) is allied to major defence contractors, while the Department of Labor works with the trade unions. The regulators (the departments) need the regulated (interest groups) for ideas and for information on how policies are working, which bind both closely together. Clientele groups can also press agency claims in Congress and so act as an alternative link between bureaucracy and the legislature. This phenomenon is further explored in Chapter 10.

Finally, it is important to realise that the federal bureaucracy is not a monolithic structure. Each bureau seeks to maintain its share of the financial and political resources of the department; thus bureaux are in competition for relatively scarce commodities.

The problem of control of the bureaucracy is very complex. The Constitution divides responsibility between President and Congress, and federal buraucrats, who are expert politicans, take advantage of this. Bureaux also seek to maximise support for their policies among the groups they are supposed to regulate. Various Presidents, in attempts to improve administrative efficiency and to exercise greater political control, have met with resistance in other parts of the political system. Congressmen fear that greater central political control changes the balance of power between the executive and legislative branches of government in favour of the President. Meanwhile, any new governmental activity usually leads to an increase in the number of agencies and the problems of control by either President or Congress become more formidable.

The problem of bureaucratic control

Although President Reagan may have wished to curb the growth of the federal establishment, bureaucratic growth, in terms of staffing, arguably is not the real problem. Even though there has been a great expansion in federal government activity in many spheres of the social and economic life of the nation, this has been achieved without the creation of a vast federal government infrastructure to administer these programmes. (Civilian employment in the federal government increased from 2.1 million in 1950 to 2.7 million in 1983.) Instead the federal government has preferred to act through well-established intermediate organisations.

1. State and city government   Local government takes responsibility for implementing many federal government projects such as road building, public housing, environmental protection, grants for mass transit systems, education and urban development. Many of these grants have tripled since the 1960s, as has employment in state and city government.

2. Private sector   Many federally funded projects are implemented by the private sector. For example Medicare and Medicaid funds are handled by hospitals and other agencies not under the direction of the federal government.

The real problem of the bureaucratic growth has not been in terms of employees but in terms of functions and finances. Since 1960 the federal budget has increased sixfold, a doubling in real terms. Both the President and Congress find it difficult to restrict both.

Political control of an expanding federal government
One of the important consequences of expanded governmental activity is that an increased number in society receive benefits. State governments benefit in terms of road-construction programmes, city governments benefit from housing and renewal projects, individuals benefit from cash payments from social welfare schemes (unemployment, old age pensions, etc.). They in turn have led the beneficiaries to become 'clients' of the federal government and like most clients they wish to protect their interests; thus they form into interest groups to represent their views to government and lobby elected officials. Government employees administering programmes seek ways of expanding and improving service provision to their clients and often form self-interested alliances to protect themselves. This results in

pressure being placed on both the President and members of Congress to maintain specific programmes.

Political control of an expanding federal budget

Perhaps more formidable for politicians is controlling federal expenditure. The doubling in real terms of the federal budget since 1960 is due almost totally to the rise in cost of existing programmes, particularly in the area of social welfare. For example, in 1960 welfare programmes accounted for about 20 per cent (or $22 thousand million) of the federal budget; by fiscal year 1990 this will rise to over 43 per cent (or $500 thousand million). Because many federal government benefits are increased at the rate of inflation, some 75 per cent of each year's budget increase is explained by the rising costs of existing programmes.

The political difficulty that politicians face on this issue, which also illustrates the power of client groups, could, for example, be seen when President Reagan announced in 1982 that he wished to make certain cuts in welfare payments to senior citizens. Such was the public outcry in the country and Congress against these cuts, made at a time when the President was inceasing defence expenditure, that Reagan was forced to reconsider his proposals.

The increasing budget deficits in the 1980s, however, led Congress to pass the Balanced Budget and Emergency Deficit Control Act (Gramm–Rudman–Hollings). This stipulates that the budget deficit be lowered by a specific amount each year until the budget is balanced in fiscal year 1991. If Congress does not meet the mandated deficit in any year, across-the-board cuts are made on every budget head. In 1986 4.3 per cent was cut from every programme, except those specifically exempted by Congress, which included social security and Reagan's Strategic Defense Initiative. Gramm–Rudman–Hollings indicates that politicians are prepared to act to control the increasing federal budget, but are wary of making cuts in such politically sensitive areas as social security.

The problem that both the President and Congress face with budgetary control of the bureaucracy is that they are not the only political actors. Both share political power with a large number of interest groups which have developed following the increase in governmental intervention in society. Control of the bureaucracy may be difficult for elected officials, but the bureaucracy is not unresponsive to interest groups and public opinion, which can also exert control through pressure on politicians. The pluralistic nature of the American political system, with its many access points, means also that it is difficult to reduce the size and scope of bureaucratic activity. The bureaucracy will survive because it performs the service which many in society want and need, and both the President and Congressmen understand this bare fact of politics.

Further reading

H. Helco, 'Issue Networks and the Executive Establishment', in A. King (ed.), *The New American System*, American Enterprise Institute, 1978.

F. E. Rourke, *Bureaucracy, Politics and Public Policy*, 3rd edn, Little, Brown, 1984.

H. Seidman, *Politics, Position and Power: The Dynamics of Federal Organization*, 3rd edn, Oxford University Press, 1980.

Questions

1. How effective are presidential and congressional controls on the federal bureaucracy?

2. Account for the expansion of the federal bureaucracy in the last three decades.

10

THE MAKING OF PUBLIC POLICY

The view from the nineties

As the twentieth century draws to a close, there is a perceptible and growing concern over what the future holds for the United States. A great deal of this worry is focused on what is seen as the relative decline of the United States. The United States, which has been the most powerful and wealthy nation in the world for the past half-century, is no longer in such a dominant position. Moreover, there are strong reasons to believe that its position is likely to be eroded even further. Interestingly, the threat to American dominance has not emerged from the nation that successive American administrations, since the end of the Second World War, have most feared, the USSR. The USSR suffers, if anything, from far more substantial problems and difficulties. The competition that Americans increasingly fear comes from Japan and the nations of the Pacific Rim, such as South Korea, Taiwan and, perhaps in the not too distant future, China. American concerns in this regard are located primarily in the economic arena and the apparent inability of the United States to compete as effectively as it has done in the past. Virtually every economic indicator suggests that the American economy has not functioned as well as that of Japan, or even of several Western European nations, for instance, France and Germany. The political context of the 1990s will be that of the relative economic decline of the United States and whether this relative decline can be arrested.

But why has this relative economic decline come about? Of course, most of the suggested causes are located in the structure of the American economy and are not of any particular interest to the concerns of this book. There are several reasons, however, which are broadly political. For instance, the economy has suffered from a higher incidence of illiteracy and innumeracy amongst those who graduate from secondary school than other Western nations. In other words, the education system, especially in the inner cities, has not provided a work-force which is appropriate for the requirements of a very sophisticated economy. Too many Americans are passing through the school system without achieving a satisfactory education and learning the necessary skills for an internationally competitive economy. Moreover, there is an imbalance in the skills that are learned; there is for instance, a shortage of engineers, which hinders the progress of the manufacturing sector of the economy. So if the inadequacy of the education system has been one of the contributory factors in the relative decline of the American economy, can it be remedied? The answer to this question, however, does raise very substantial questions about the nature of the American political process.

If Americans are to begin the process of arresting this relative decline, let alone reversing it, then there is going to have to be a concerted effort to reform several of those practices and some of the behaviour that has brought about the problem. So the key questions for the next decade concern the response of the policy-making process to this set of economic difficulties. Can the public policy-making process devise a solution to the problems besetting the American economy? Can the President, Congress and the federal bureaucracy, over the next few years, construct and implement a package of measures that will restore vitality and dynamism to the American economy? It is difficult, unfortunately, to answer these questions with any degree of optimism.

The policy-making process in the United States looks increasingly problematic. There appears to be a very real inability on the part of the institutions of the federal government to deal with these very pressing difficulties and problems that confront the United States. Let us take a current example of an apparently insuperable problem, the federal budget deficit: a problem which in view of many economists has been a very significant factor in the economic difficulties of the past decade. The federal budget deficit has been responsible, in part, for pushing up and then maintaining a high level of interest rates. It has contributed to a record US balance of trade deficit and has been a destabilising factor in the world economy. But yet the policy-making process has yet to deal with the budget deficit.

As we have seen in Chapter 5, the deficit emerged during the Reagan administration. President Reagan persuaded the Congress, during his first year in office, to reduce the levels of taxation and increase defence expenditure simultaneously. However, he failed to convince the Congress to make sufficient and proportionate reductions in non-defence expenditures, with the result that a substantial and apparently unbridgable gap between the federal government's revenues and expenditures appeared. But the responsibility for this state of affairs must not be placed solely on the Reagan administration, nor should the Bush administration be seen to have exclusive responsibility for the deficit. The Congress, of course, had and continues to share the responsibility with the executive branch for the continuation of a budget deficit that is seen, by most observers, as damaging to the health of both the American and world economies. The failure to deal with the deficit over the past several years cannot be explained satisfactorily by the personality of Presidents Reagan or Bush. Nor can it be located exclusively in the office of the presidency, or within the executive branch, or for that matter within the Congress. It is, in fact, a failure of the the policy-making process in the United States. So why has this occurred, why has the policy-making process failed to control the deficit? Unfortunately this is a question that is not easily answered, but nevertheless an answer must be attempted.

The policy-making process

To a considerable extent the failure of the policy-making process in controlling the deficit during the 1980s is an indication or a more general and deep-seated malaise in the American political process, a malaise that has been evident for some considerable time but which has been exacerbated by recent developments. This combination of recent developments and long-established procedures and practices has heightened concerns about the American political process and its seeming inability to make policy both effectively and with relative dispatch. There follow some of the most significant characteristics of the current American policy-making process.

The constitutional structure
The policy-making process in the United States operates within an eighteenth-century constitutional structure. As we have seen in

Chapter 1, the Founding Fathers were anxious to create a political system that did not make policy effectively or quickly. Their principal fear was of government, its power and the abuse of that power. Consequently, they deliberately set out in design a political structure, where governmental power was fragmented. They wanted to ensure that it would be difficult for the institutions of the federal government to act in concert. They hoped that the relations between the executive, legislative and judicial branches would be characterised by a persistent antagonism if not open hostility, and to a considerable extent their hopes have been fulfilled. Moreover, the Founding Fathers wanted a policy-making process with innumerable points of access, where interests, however small, not only could make their views known but would also affect the decisions being taken. The delegates, who met in Philadelphia in 1787, wanted an extended, slow and cumbersome decision-making process and they achieved their objective.

The decline of the political parties
The fragmentation of governmental power has been a constant factor in American politics since 1787. However, this fragmentation had been mitigated, to a considerable extent, by the presence of political parties. The Founding Fathers were profoundly suspicious of parties and it was their fervent hope that parties would not emerge on the American political landscape. But they did emerge, and one of the consequences of their existence is that parties have provided a degree of cement in this fragmented political process. As we have seen in Chapter 7, the political party has modified the intentions of the Founding Fathers. If the same party controls both the presidency and the Congress, then the degree of conflict between the two has on the whole diminished and from time to time might even be replaced by co-operation. Of course, there have been several examples of bitter intra-party conflict. For instance, during the latter part of the New Deal, President Franklin D. Roosevelt was confronted by intense opposition from sections within his own Democratic Party, and more recently President Carter did not have especially good relations with his fellow Democrats in the Congress. Nevertheless, party loyalty was an important factor in the success of the early New Deal legislative programme between 1933 and 1937. Similarly, the passage of President Lyndon Johnson's Great

Society legislation in 1965 and 1966 was due to the enthusiastic support of congressional Democrats. Even President Reagan, at least during the first term in office, was able to rally most of the Republicans in the Congress behind his administration, but this appeared to be more the exception than the rule, for there is little doubt that the connections and loyalties of party are diminishing. So why has role of party diminished in Washington?

As already noted in Chapter 7, the reasons for the decline of party are numerous. Party organisations have atrophied in many areas of the nation. Parties no longer control the process of nomination. Parties, to a considerable extent, have been replaced by candidates. Individual candidates raise their own finance, hire their own coalition of support within their consistuency. In other words, the success of a candidate pretty much depends on their personal abilities and efforts, and on the coalition of supporters they have assembled locally. The consequence of this development is that after the election Senators or Representatives have few obligations to their party. They have been elected in their own right and their success has not been dependent on national party affiliations but on local factors. Consequently politicians look to their constitutency and not to their party leadership in the Congress or the White House: they look to the periphery and not to the centre. Therefore Presidents increasingly have a difficult task in acquiring the support of members of their own party. There is no guarantee that Republicans in the Senate and the House of Representatives will support President Bush's legislative programme: indeed, it can be predicted safely that a very significant proportion will not vote for a percentage of the President's proposals.

Interest groups
Chapter 8 noted the very wide range of interest groups that exist in the United States and the extent of their activities. One of the striking characteristics of current American politics is this extraordinary array of groups and their importance in the policymaking process. To some extent, interest groups have moved into the gap created by the decline of the political parties. They are important sources of both information and finance. Through the development of the PAC, interest groups have become very important players in the election process and as a consequence they are listened to by the successful candidate when he or she

takes up office in Washington. They are far more persuasive in the Washington of today than they were in the conditions of a few decades ago. They are more persuasive because their influence is not counterbalanced by the political parties, at least not to the extent that it was only twenty or thirty years previously. Then the Democratic and Republican Parties provided a degree of protection between a Senator or Representative and the lobbying of interest groups, but that protective barrier now has been substantially reduced. The result of this growth in the importance of interest groups in Washington has been profound.

Because interest groups are, in the main, narrowly and specifically focused, they do not, on the whole, pursue matters of a wider and more general concern. They primarily are anxious to achieve their more limited goals. The Democratic and Republican Parties, by contrast, historically have pursued the broader picture. They have sought to promote, if you like, the general welfare, while the interest groups have been concerned with the welfare of their own members. This is a very important distinction. Both parties and interest groups are vital and essential elements for the satisfactory operation of a democratic political process, but in the United States the relationship between them appears to have altered over the past decades. One of the most important consequences of this alteration in their relationship is that the policy-making process is far more responsive to the demands of the interest groups. The general welfare is not represented as effectively in Washington as the specific concerns of the interest groups.

So if these are the principal characteristics of the policy-making process, how has this process grappled with the federal budget deficit during the 1980s?

The federal budget deficit

One of the striking aspects of the federal budget deficit is that all the principal political actors in Washington, throughout the past decade, have been in agreement. Presidents Reagan and Bush constantly have declared their worries over the deficit and the damaging impact that it will have on the economy. The leaders of the two parties, in both the Senate and the House of Representatives, also have frequently stated their concerns about the deficit and moreover have committed themselves to its removal. But the deficit has continued, apparently well able to resist the combined opposition of the parties and of the executive and legislative branches of government. Even those measures that have been enacted to control and reduce the deficit have not been effective. So why has the deficit been so difficult to eliminate?

1. It is politically easy to reduce taxes The proposals by the Reagan administration to lower tax rates in 1981 and again in 1986 were widely welcomed. The enthusiasm for tax reductions, in part, was based on a widespread sense, especially in 1981, that tax rates were too high. However, in general there is little political mileage to be had out of opposing lower taxes. Consequently there was no opposition by the Democrats in the Congress to reducing taxes. There were disagreements over who should be the principal beneficiaries of the tax cuts, but not over the broad intention to lower taxes. On the whole politicians are only too anxious to reduce the taxes of their constituents. On occasion, however, some politicians have called for taxes to be increased to reduce the deficit, but their record of electoral success has not been impressive. The most notable figure to do so was Walter Mondale, the Democratic presidential candidate in 1984, and, of course, he suffered an extremely heavy electoral defeat at the hands of President Reagan. Very noticeably, Michael Dukakis, the Democratic candidate in 1988, refused to make any similar suggestions, while George Bush made his attitude very clear with the most frequently repeated remark of the campaign, 'Read my lips, no new taxes.' There are now organised interests, with any power and influence, that endorse higher taxes. Consequently, the vast majority of politicians have distanced themselves from embracing proposals for higher taxes, even though there may well be very sound reasons for such an increase.

2. It is politically difficult to reduce expenditures If tax increases were politically impossible, the only alternative to reducing the deficit was and is to reduce federal expenditures. Unfortunately, this has proved to be almost as difficult as increasing taxes. In part the problems have been compounded by the fact that defence spending, which constitutes approximately one-third of the federal expenditure, was protected. It was protected not only by the administration but by a very influential series of interests determined to maintain a large military establishment in the United

States. It is often referred to as the military/industrial complex, which is composed primarily of the large manufacturers of defence equipment, the military and their allies. In fact, the Reagan administration did not only wish to maintain the existing levels of defence spending, it proposed and the Congress passed very substantial increases in defence expenditures, which meant that the onus of reductions had to be placed on non-defence spending and, in particular, those items which required congressional approval each year. (There is a category of items which cannot be adjusted annually, such as the interest on the National Debt, and which also amounts to one-third of federal expenditures.) So if the budget was to be balanced, those programmes, in housing, education and welfare, would have had to be either terminated or reduced in scope quite dramatically. Neither of these scenarios came to pass, because there were, once again, powerful interest groups which were committed to the continuance of these programmes. They lobbied extensively and effectively for their maintenance and the Congress responded by refusing to to impose the full level of spending reductions on these programmes. The result of this congressional refusal, of course, was that the budget deficit continued.

3. *The choice of the politically safe option* Faced with the impasse of the deficit, the Congress chose to pass the Balanced Budget and Emergency Deficit Control Act (Gramm–Rudman–Hollings) in December 1985. The objective of Gramm–Rudman–Hollings was to eliminate the deficit over a period of years. In each year from 1986 to 1991, the Act requires $36 billion of expenditure reductions in order to bring the budget into balance. However, the Act very deliberately sought to protect the politicians from making the difficult choices that would have to be made if that figure was to be met. Gramm–Rudman–Hollings, quite extraordinarily, delegated the responsibility of deciding where the expenditure axe was to fall to the United States Comptroller General. It was such an extraordinary procedure that it was challenged in the courts as being unconstitutional, and in fact the Supreme Court did find it thus. The Supreme Court returned this responsibility to the Congress, which has exercised it in such a manner as to minimise political difficulties. The spending reductions required by Gamm–Rudman–Hollings, have been achieved to a considerable extent by financial skill and accounting procedures rather than by imposing spending cuts, which would have caused real political problems with the interest groups concerned. Gramm–Rudman–Hollings has not, to date at least, achieved its objective, because the policymaking process has refused to grasp the very difficult issues contained in eliminating the deficit.

Conclusion

The problems with controlling the federal budget deficit suggest that the American policy-making process is unable to confront a very difficult and awkward problem. It has not done so for the reasons outlined above. The parties are weak; the constitutional procedures are complex; the members of Congress are constantly looking over their shoulders to the voters back home; the interest groups are omnipresent; there is no representation of the national interest. In Chapter 8, competing explanations over who rules America were noted, but perhaps the inability to eliminate the budget deficit almost suggests that nobody rules America. There are almost too many interests to take into account, too many views that have too be considered, so that the policy-making process ceases to deal with the nation's problems. The American political process is characterised, one might say, by a hyper-pluralism, with such a range of interests that participate and effectively participate, that the policy-makers are unable to take decisive actions. Instead they hesitate and temporise and hope that they can avoid taking the difficult decisions. Unfortunately, the next decade and beyond does not look especially promising for the United States. The problems associated with its relative decline will not disappear and difficult decisions will have to be taken even if the United States is going to arrest, if not reverse, its position. But if it is going to do so, the policy-making process is going to have to perform far more effectively than it has during the 1980s.

Further reading

Richard Maidment and John Zvesper (eds.), *Reflections on the Constitution: The American Constitution After Two Hundred Years*, Manchester University Press, 1989.

Paul E. Peterson, 'The New Politics of Deficits', in John E.

Chubb and Paul E. Peterson (eds.), *The New Directions in American Politics*, The Brookings Institution, 1985.

Nelson, W. Polsby, *Political Innovations in America: The Politics of Policy Initiation*, Yale University Press, 1983.

James A. Thurber, 'Budgetary Continuity and Change: An Assessment of the Congressional Budget Process', in D. K. Adams (ed.), *Studies in US Politics*, Manchester University Press, 1989.

Questions

1. Describe and analyse the problems of the American policy-making process.

2. Why has the federal budget deficit been so difficult to eliminate?

11

VOTERS AND ELECTIONS

Introduction

Recent political history suggests that with victories in five of the last six presidential elections the Republican Party have achieved an electoral lock on the White House. The only Democratic Party victory, in 1976 by Jimmy Carter, could, in part, be explained by special circumstances following Watergate. Yet from 1932 to 1964, in nine presidential elections, the position was reversed, with the Democratic candidates victorious in seven and the Republicans winning only two, 1952 and 1956, with Second World War hero Dwight Eisenhower as their standard-bearer. Again it might be argued special circumstances prevailed.

Not only have the Republicans achieved greater success in the number of presidential contests since 1968 but, as Table 11.1 indicates, the margin of victory, in both the popular vote and electoral college vote, has been substantial.

What explains the decline of the Democratic Party and the resurgence of the Republican Party in presidential election contests since 1968? Despite the fact that most voters still see themselves as Democrats, has the era of Democratic domination of American politics, which began with the election of Franklin Roosevelt in 1932, come to an end? Is the Republican Party in the 1980s emerging as the 'natural' party of government in the United States?

To answer these questions and to understand why change is happening we have to look closely at five interrelated factors.

(a) The historical basis of the present party voting coalitions, or the long-term forces which have an effect on presidential elections.

(b) Physical changes in the electorate.

Table 11.1 Presidential election results 1960–88

| | % popular vote | | Electoral college votes | | |
	Dem.	Rep.	Dem.	Rep.	Other
1960	49.7	49.5	303	219	15
1964	61.1	38.5	486	52	0
1968	42.7	43.4	191	301	46
1972	37.5	60.7	17	520	1
1976	50.1	48.0	297	240	1
1980	41.0	50.7	49	489	0
1984	40.6	58.8	13	525	0
1988	45.5	54.5	112	426	0

(*c*) Party identification – or the social-psychological attachment to a political party.

(*d*) Short-term factors which affect particular election contests.

(*e*) Changes in the way in which presidential elections are conducted.

The historical background

The origin of the present party voting coalitions is to be found, in part, in the politics of the 1930s. The Great Depression, which followed the Wall Street Crash in 1929, brought to the White House in 1932 the first Democratic Party President for twelve years, Franklin D. Roosevelt. In the 1930s the Roosevelt administration attempted to tackle the massive problems of unemployment and social dislocation by using the power of the federal government to create jobs, provide welfare and to rebuild the economy in the aftermath of the Great Depression. Simultaneously Roosevelt created a new Democratic Party voting coalition in the electorate composed primarily of the South, Northern city dwellers (mainly working class, trade unionists, Catholic and black) and Western farmers, which gave his party a succession of presidential election victories from 1932 to 1948. In the minds of the American electorate the Democratic Party from that time has been seen as the party prepared to use the power of the federal government:

(*a*) to regulate economic activity mainly through budget deficit financing to maintain full employment;

(*b*) to take responsibility for the social welfare of its citizens by providing unemployment benefits, health insurance schemes and other forms of assistance;

(*c*) to follow an internationalist foreign policy and involve the United States actively in world affairs.

If the Democrats in the 1930s were identified as the party which used the power of the federal government to regulate the economy, the view of the Republican Party in the minds of the electorate can be seen as a mirror image of their adversaries. The Republicans, because they controlled the presidency and Congress at the time of the Wall Street Crash were held responsible for the Great Depression, and for the ideology and policies which brought it about. Thus the Republicans were perceived by voters as the party which supported:

(*a*) economic *laissez-faire* capitalism, and believed that business enterprise should be regulated by market forces;

(*b*) the idea that individuals in society should be responsible for the provision of their own welfare benefits through the private sector;

(*c*) the idea that an 'isolationist' foreign policy be pursued and that the United States should not get involved in foreign entanglements.

These generalised images of both political parties, with the major exception of Republican foreign policy attitudes, lasted throughout the 1950s and 1960s. When the Republicans won the presidency in 1952 there was no major dismantling of the corporate state established by previous Democratic administrations, and broad Republican acceptance of regulation by the federal government saw a gradual diminution of party differences in this area of public policy.

However, in the 1960s and early 1970, major changes started to take place in the issue agenda of American politics with black civil rights, US involvement in Vietnam, and the question of individual lifestyles challenging economic questions as the electorate's major concerns. These new issues particularly divided the Democratic Party, as we shall see, and can partially explain the decline of the party's support among the electorate.

As the United States entered the 1980s, economic and foreign policy issues returned as major public concerns. But it is the Republicans, and not the Democrats, at the presidential level who are perceived as handling these issues more effectively. This can be related to President Carter's inept management of the economy, where both unemployment and inflation increased, and the setbacks he suffered in foreign affairs, particularly in Iran and Afghanistan.

By contrast, at the end of Reagan's first administration in 1984 both the unemployment and inflation rates had fallen, and the United States had begun to take a tougher stand against liberation movements in Central America. Relations with the Soviet Union, the 'Evil Empire', as President Reagan designated it, also became more confrontational, as the United States increased its defence budget to meet the perceived Soviet challenge.

In the second term, optimism among the electorate continued. More than 50 per cent of Americans thought themselves to be better off in 1988 than four years previously. Inflation and unemployment continued to fall in an economy which had created 11 million new jobs in the decade. Concerns were expressed about the budget and trade deficits but these were considered of less importance than the new issues of drugs and crime. In his relations with the Soviet Union, President Reagan changed tack and began to negotiate on arms control. In March 1985 Mikhail Gorbachev took over in the Kremlin and by November he and Reagan had met in Geneva to discuss the reduction of medium-range nuclear weapons in Europe. By 1986 they had met again in Reykjavik and Moscow, and finally Washington in 1988 to sign the INF Treaty.

By the end of the Reagan presidency the economy was stronger, despite budget and trade deficits, and a *rapprochement* had been achieved with the Soviet Union. As Ronald Reagan said, 'America *is* back *and* standing tall.'

From the 1930s to almost the 1990s the political wheel has turned full circle. The Democrats are no longer seen as the party of prosperity and the Republicans the party of depression. The public approval ratings of President Reagan's handling of the economy and US–Soviet relations (and the electorate's memory of the inability of Jimmy Carter to cope with these problems), have blurred the perceptions that voters have had about both parties and have thus affected the party loyalties of the American voter.

Physical change in the electorate

The composition of the American electorate is affected by two factors: legal requirements as to who is entitled to vote, and the physical replacement of the electorate.

The regulation of the franchise

Until the passage of the 1965 Voting Rights Act each state was left, subject to certain limitations imposed by the Constitution, national legislation and the Supreme Court, to determine its own electoral laws. This enabled many states, particularly in the South, to prevent blacks and other minorities voting, which they accomplished through poll taxes, literacy tests and grandfather clauses (forebears were slaves). The Twenty-fourth Amend- ment to the Constitution abolished poll taxes and the 1965 Act enabled federal government officials to register voters in states where literacy tests were used. The impact of these reforms can easily be seen. In Alabama, before the passage of the Voting Rights Act, only 19.3 per cent of blacks were registered to vote; by 1969 this figure had risen to 51.6 per cent. In Mississippi the increase was even more noteworthy. Before the Act 6.7 per cent were registered, by 1968, 59.8 per cent. By 1980, black registration was only 10 per cent below the figure for whites.

The size of the electorate was further increased in 1970 with the passage of the Voting Rights Act Amendment which enfranchised 18-year-olds for federal elections, and in 1971 by the Twenty-sixth Amendment which extended this to all elections, increasing the electorate by 11 million by 1972.

The final reform which eased voter access to the polls was the abolition of residency requirements and the easing of registration procedures by the 1970 Act. Until that time 38 states required at least a year's residence before a voter could register. The Act imposed a thirty-day residency requirement for presidential elections. In a nation which has a highly mobile population, particularly among the young and the affluent, these relexations should encourage more participation in voting by these groups.

Further attempted reform of the registration process by the Carter administration in 1977 to allow election-day registration was defeated in Congress.

However, the US voter registration is low. In 1980 it was estimated that about 40 per cent of the electorate was unregistered or more than 60 million from an electorate of 159 million. The reason for low voter registration is that the onus rests with the individual. Unlike the United Kingdom where the government takes responsibility for compiling a list of registered voters, in the United States neither the state nor federal governments perform this task.

The physical replacement of the electorate

This occurs through older voters dying and new voters coming of age. One political scientist has estimated that 25 per cent of the electorate is replaced every decade.

The physical replacement of the electorate has important but differing implications for party voting coalitions. By the mid-1980s, those voters who participated in politics for the first time during the New Deal era, and who formed the backbone of the Democratic Party voting coalition, were a diminishing proportion of the electorate. Their demise reduces the number of voters who support the values of the New Deal, particularly the pivotal role of the federal government in managing the economy and supporting social welfare programmes.

These older electors are being replaced by younger and generally better-educated voters, but voters who are less inclined to participate in politics and less inclined to have strong party ties. For example, in 1972 only 53 per cent in the 18–24 age group voted, compared to 74 per cent of those aged 33–39. But more importantly, younger voters are changing their party allegiance. In 1980 Carter polled 44 per cent of the 18–29 age group against Reagan's 43 per cent. In 1984 Reagan won more than 59 per cent of this age group's votes, and Bush led Dukakis in 1988 by 52 per cent to 47 per cent. These figures indicate that the Republicans are undermining what has been in past presidential elections Democratic Party support. Secondly, the GOP appears to be in the process of laying the foundations of a new voting coalition based in part on those voters who came of age in the 1970s and 80s who witnessed the failure of Democratic Presidents to cope with the economic and international problems facing the United States and being led by a Republican one that could.

Party identification

Early studies of voting behaviour in the United States emphasised social characteristics like class, age, occupation and religion as important factors in influencing the party choice of individual electors. But in the 1960s a number of studies were published which argued that voting behaviour could be best explained by an individual's *psychological* orientation to politics. Respondents to national surveys were questioned on their attitudes to parties, candidates and tʰ ֵ political issues of the day, and from the data collected researchers were able to build a picture of how people thought about politics. The most important measure developed in these studies is the concept of *party identification* or partisanship, which is an individual's 'psychological commitment or attachment to a political party'. Party identification represents a feeling of sympathy for and loyalty to a political party that develops in childhood through political socialisation, and itensifies the longer the commitment to party is maintained. However, although partisanship may lead the voter to support that party at the polls, it is not the same as voting for the party, for events pertinent to a particular election may induce, for example, a Democratic Party identifier to cast his ballot for a Republican presidential candidate.

Table 11.2 clearly shows that the Democratic Party since 1952 has maintained a clear lead over the Republicans in terms of the distribution of partisan loyalty in the electorate. However, in this period Democratic support has declined from 57 per cent in 1952 to 53 per cent in 1980, while Republican support has fallen from only 34 per cent to 33 per cent. What is important is the decline in the percentage of voters who see themselves as strong partisans of either party, and the increased percentage of voters who have no attachment to either the Democrats or the Republicans – that is they see themselves as independents. The major increase in the number of independent identifiers occurred between 1964 and 1972, and overall this increase was paralleled by the decline in the number of Democratic partisans. The major source of the increase in independents is found in new voters. One political scientist estimated that 32 per cent of the 21–24-year-olds could be thus classified in 1964, but by 1980 this figure had risen to over 60 per cent. In addition, an anlaysis of this age group partisan attachment reveals that only 8 per cent saw themselves as strong Democrats or Republicans in 1980, while of those over 70, 44 per cent could be so classified.

By 1984, 39 per cent of the 18–24-year-old cohort declared themselves as Republican Party identifiers as against 34 per cent

Table 11.2 Party identification 1952–88

	Democrat			Independent	Republican			Apolitical
	Strong	Weak	Independent		Independent	Weak	Strong	
1952	22	25	10	5	7	14	13	4
1956	21	23	7	9	8	14	15	3
1960	21	25	8	8	7	13	14	4
1964	27	25	9	8	6	13	11	2
1968	20	25	10	10	0	15	10	2
1972	15	26	11	13	10	13	10	2
1976	15	25	12	14	10	14	9	2
1980	18	23	12	13	10	14	9	2
1984	18	22	10	7	13	15	14	2
1988	15	21	12	13	13	16	9	2

Source: National Election Studies data available through Inter-University Consortium for Political and Social Research, University of Michigan; adapted from Table 1 in J. Fishel, *Parties and Elections in an Anti-Party Age*, Indiana University Press, 1978, p. xxi. Percentages are rounded up and do not all total 100 per cent.

for the Democrats, while more impressively 60 per cent of this cohort voted for Reagan.

These figures suggest a bleak future for the Democratic Party. While Democrats in 1984 held a 3:2 advantage over Republicans among party identifiers, independents became a larger part of the population. This evidence suggests that there is a long-term decline in party loyalty, with the Democrats, as the majority party, suffering most. Despite most voters seeing themselves as Democrats, from 1968 to 1984 the latter have, as noted before, lost five of the six presidential election contests. An explanation why the Republicans have been in the ascendant in this period might be the short-term factors which are relevant to particular election contests.

Short-term factors which affect elections

As well as the long-term forces like party identification there are also particular events pertinent to each election which have an impact on voting behaviour and which might account for departures from prevailing party loyalties. These short-term forces are the presidential candidates themselves and the issues specific to each election.

The impact of presidential candidates
For any political party the choice of the presidential candidate is important. This is particularly so for the Republicans, as only a minority of voters identify with them; hence if they are to win an election they must attract support from voters who see themselves as independents or Democrats. Consequently the image that a candidate creates in the voters' minds is of paramount importance.

There is little doubt that the personal appeal of Eisenhower in 1952 and 1956 as being 'above party politics' enabled the Republicans to win the presidency for the first time since 1928, by attracting votes of Democratic identifiers who at the same time retained their partisanship by supporting Democrats for Congress. Conversely, even Republican supporters deserted Barry Goldwater in 1964, as he was seen as being too conservative. Learning from this, the Reagan campaign managers in 1980 and again in 1984 sought to dissassociate their candidate from the conservative positions of many of his followers. In the last election President Reagan particularly sought to broaden his appeal to independents and Democrats by quoting past Democratic Party presidents like Franklin Roosevelt and John Kennedy.

The actions of Democratic Party nominees for the presidency have also driven its party identifiers into the Republican camp. In 1972, George McGovern's ineptitude in handling the selection of his running mate, combined with his vacillation on campaign issues, tarnished his image as an effective politician and led many traditional Democratic voters to abstain or support Nixon. Similarly in 1984 Walter Mondale's honesty about raising taxes to cope with the budget deficit and his problems with his running-mate Geraldine Ferraro helped Reagan take 26 per cent of Democratic Party identifiers and over 60 per cent of independents.

Issues and presidential elections 1952–84

The nine presidential elections held since 1952 have taken place in a diverse period of American history. The Eisenhower presidency of the 1950s can be characterised as a relatively tranquil period politically. The Republican Party accepted many of the economic and social reforms of the New Deal and, in a time of full employment and economic growth, the problem of the domestic economy, which had been paramount in the 1930s, was of secondary concern to the electorate. The most important political issues in the 1950s were those connected with foreign policy: the Cold War, the bomb and the threat of communism. However, foreign policy issues did not seem to affect voters directly and were not politically divisive; the American public felt that in Eisenhower they had a President well able to maintain the peace.

The lack of relative political conflict in the 1950s and the broad acceptance by the Republicans of the New Deal reforms led many commentators to suggest that the country was moving into an era where ideology in politics played little part. Indeed one survey demonstrated that only 3.5 per cent of voters could be said to think of politics in terms of broad political principles such as liberalism and conservatism.

However, with the onset of the 1960s the pattern changed, and the country entered a relatively turbulent period politically. The presidencies of Kennedy, Johnson and Nixon saw the rise of new issues: racial equality, the Vietnam War and crime, drugs and the problems of youth. These issues were important because they deeply affected the public in that they cut across the party divisions associated with the economic and social welfare issues of the New Deal.

What impact did these issues have on the Democratic and Republican party voting coalitions?

1. Racial equality The question of racial integration is probably the most divisive issue in post-war American politics. Democratic Party identification with black demands for civil rights was illustrated when President Johnson vigorously supported legislation to outlaw racial discrimination. The consequences of a Democratic Party President associating himself and his party with the cause of racial equality led gradually to the loss of white Southern support for the party in the 1964 elections, the George Wallace candidacy in 1968, and the emergence of Southern Republicanism in subsequent presidential contests. In 1952 about 70 per cent of white Southerners saw themselves as Democrats, and fewer than 20 per cent Republicans. By 1984 white Southerners were only 37 per cent Democrats and 34 per cent Republican. The dominance of the GOP, particularly in the Deep South, can be seen in the 1984 elections where Reagan won majorities of 62 per cent in Mississippi and Louisiana and 60 per cent in Alabama.

Although the Democratic Party lost white support for its presidential candidates in the South, by the end of the 1960s it had the solid support of the black electorate. By 1980, 81 per cent of blacks were Democratic Party identifiers, and 85 per cent voted for Jimmy Carter. By 1984, black support for the Democratic presidential candidate had risen to 90 per cent.

The impact of racial integration of the voting coalition of both parties was also evidenced outside the South, where many blue-collar industrial workers in the North felt that Democratic Party presidential candidates had neglected their concerns and were now targeting their policies on minority groups. The loss of blue-collar support by the Democratic Party can be seen in 1984 when 53 per cent of this group voted for Ronald Reagan.

2. Vietnam Unlike racial integration, which has occupied a central position in American politics from the mid-1960s to the present day, American involvement in Vietnam was a major campaign issue only in 1968 and 1972. In 1968 American policy in

Vietnam divided leading Democratic Party politicians, and Eugene McCarthy's success in the New Hampshire primary eventually led Lyndon Johnson not to seek a second term as President. In the aftermath of a rancorous party convention in Chicago, Hubert Humphrey attempted to take an independent position on Vietnam to encourage liberal Democratic dissidents to return to the fold. Although he was partially successful, the Democratic Party was perceived by voters to be divided on the issue and this internal division contributed to the Democrats' defeat in the November elections.

In 1972 the division *between* the parties over Vietnam was more clear-cut. McGovern advocated a policy of withdrawal, while Nixon pursued a strategy of a negotiated 'peace with honour'. Pomper has found (in G. Pomper and S. E. Lederman, *Elections in America*, Longman, 2nd edn, 1980) that young Democrats who supported withdrawal were virtually unanimous in their vote for McGovern, while one-quarter of the older voters chose Nixon even though they were both Democrats and 'doves'. At the same time, a high proportion of blue-collar workers and working-class Democrats deserted to Nixon.

The Vietnam issue in 1968 and 1972 had the effect of weakening party ties, particularly in the Democratic Party voting coalition. In 1968 party leadership was divided on the issue and gave no clear signals to its supporters, and the supporters in their turn felt frustrated at the lack of a coherent policy to follow. By 1972, when there were clear differences between McGovern and Nixon on the issue, conservative Democrats supported the Nixon candidacy.

3. Lifestyle issues Research in the early 1970s showed that young voters in an affluent society were less concerned with tradition and personal economic advancement and more with non-material and personal freedoms like sexual equality, liberalisation of the marijuana laws and reform of the law on abortion. These issues came to the fore in the 1972 election, and it was widely publicised by McGovern's political opponents that the Democratic candidate supported 'amnesty, acid and abortion'. The perception, although incorrect, that McGovern supported these issues and was a political extremist further eroded his base of support in the Democratic Party. To the young, to be a 'liberal' entailed support for such personal freedoms. For the older voter 'liberalism' meant government support for full employment, and social welfare policies. To the older voter, opinions on personal freedoms were not an important part of his 'liberalism', and a division occurred again in the Democratic coalition over this issue.

Thus Nixon's emphasis in 1972 on a tough law and order policy, his acceptance of a managed economy, a negotiated peace in Vietnam and *détente* with the Soviet Union, attracted support from Democratic Party identifiers, because he and not McGovern more closely represented the liberal values they supported.

By 1976 and the Carter–Ford election, the issues of race, Vietnam and personal lifestyles, although of concern to many voters, receded into the background. Following the Arab–Israeli war of 1973 and the massive increase in oil prices, the United States' economy moved into a recession, with inflation and unemployment increasing. In foreign affairs, the major focus was again the relationship between the United States and the USSR. A third issue, in the aftermath of Watergate, was the honesty and integrity of politicians, particularly those based in Washington. Jimmy Carter placed great emphasis, in his campaign for the presidency, by running *against* Washington and for a return to morality and high standards in public life, in addition to a record of competence as a manager of government. It was difficult for a Democrat not to win, yet Carter's popular vote majority over Gerald Ford was 2 percentage points.

By 1980, Carter's reputation was in ruins.

(*a*) *Domestic policy*. The president's inability to reduce inflation and unemployment undermined the public view that the Democrats were the party better equipped to manage the economy.

(*b*) *Foreign affairs*. Despite the success of the Camp David agreement between Israel and Egypt, Carter's handling of the Iran hostage crisis and the Soviet invasion of Afghanistan led many to believe that the United States was becoming increasingly ineffective in world politics. Many felt, too, that the United States was losing military superiority over the Soviet Union which was then engaged in a massive arms build-up. The failure of the helicopter airlift of the Tehran hostages and the lack of military challenge to the Soviets' invasion of Afghanistan seemed to support this view.

(c) *The Carter style*. Although Carter's handling of these issues and his performance in office were important, also critical was the 'style' or image he presented to the electorate. Collapsing while jogging reinforced the image of a weak and ineffective president.

The poor performance of the Carter administration, particularly in the handling of economic matters, raised questions, too, about the ability of the federal government to resolve the issues of the day. One of the major principles underlying American politics since the New Deal was that the federal government should play an activist and interventionist role in society. Until 1980, differences between the Democratic and Republican parties had been about *how far* their intervention should go, now the debate centred on the question as to whether it *should* intervene. For the Democratic Party the question was more important than the *short-term* failures of Carter's administration, for it challenged a fundamental *long-term* principle held by the party: that federal government activity was beneficial to society.

By 1980, the political wheel had turned full circle. The issues that dominated debate in the 1930s, and that traditionally the Democratic Party were perceived as better at handling, were salient – but the voters not only rejected a Democratic incumbent because of poor performance in office, in favour of a *laissez-faire* conservative, but began to question validity of the principles on which the Democrats had achieved so much electoral success in the past.

In his campaign for the presidency in 1980, Ronald Reagan made two broad promises:

(a) *To reduce the role of the federal government in society*. To 'get the government off the backs' of the American people, Reagan proposed to reduce the amount of government intervention in society and secondly to reduce the levels of personal taxation. To achieve this Reagan embraced supply-side economics, through which tax cuts would stimulate investment (which would lead to the production of more goods) and less government regulation (which could again lead to an increase in productivity). The Economic Recovery Tax Act 1981 reduced tax rates by 23 per cent over three years while the highest tax rate was cut from 70 per cent to 50 per cent. The President also proposed cuts in many social welfare programmes. The blend of tax cuts, deregulation, cuts in social welfare progrmmes and increases in military expenditure became known as Reaganomics.

The success of Reagnonomics can be seen in the fall in the inflation rate from 12.4 per cent in 1980 to 3.8 per cent in 1983. Unemployment fell to 7 per cent and the Gross National Product was growing at about 9 per cent per year.

(*b*) *To restore America's position in the world.* Ronald Reagan brought to the White House a belief that the Carter administration had fundamentally weakened America's position in the world and had allowed the Soviet Union to expand its political and military influence. The new President thought that the USSR was responsible for most of the evil in the world, from the instability in Central America and Africa, to the promotion of international terrorism through its Libyan allies. Reagan believed that the best method of combating the Soviet threat was to renew American military strength. In his first term Reagan instituted a massive rearmament programme, developing particularly such high-technology weapons as the B1 and Stealth bombers, the MX missile systems and the Strategic Defense Initiative. In practice, too, Reagan flexed American muscle with the invasion of Grenada in 1983 and the bombing of Libya in reprisal for Libya's support for terrorism.

Not surprisingly President Reagan beat Walter Mondale in the 1984 election. Mondale represented the traditional New Deal wing of the Democratic Party and was a 'mainstream' party candidate who was expected to do well. By November all that Mondale could hope for was to minimise the margin of his defeat. On election day 53 per cent of the electorate voted, and Reagan achieved the expected landslide victory.

The Democratic Party coalition which has been under threat for so many presidential elections received a further setback. According to exit polls the electorate divided approximately as shown in Table 11.3.

In 1984 Reagan improved on his standing in each of the above groups of voters. In addition Reagan won decisively the conservative white South. Whereas Carter in 1980 had finished within 3

Table 11.3   1984 exit polls

	Reagan (%)	*Mondale*
Union vote	46	54
Catholics	56	44
Jews	32	66
Protestants	73	26
Under 30s	59	41
Over 60s	63	36
Men	62	37
Women	57	42
Whites	66	34
Blacks	9	90

Note: Percentages are rounded and do not all total 100 per cent.

percentage points of Reagan in seven Southern states, in 1984 Reagan carried every Southern state by 18 percentage points. A similar pattern emerges in each of the other regions. In the West and Midwest Reagan led Mondale by 18 and 22 percentage points. Only in the North-Eastern industrial states was Mondale able to stem the Republican tide, but even here, in the traditional Democratic heartland, Reagan led by 4 percentage points.

The decline in support for the Democratic Party coalition has certainly weakened the party further. While Reagan undoubtedly achieved a great personal vote, he was unable to translate this into a Republican victory in Congress.

The reasons for Reagan's victory were linked to his performance in office. Some 96 per cent of those who strongly approved of the President's general performance voted for him.

(*a*) *Domestic policy*. To voters Reagan asked the simple question. 'Do you feel better off than you were four years ago?' Some 75 per cent thought that they were financially better off or at the same level than a year before, which suggests a high degree of voter satisfaction with Reagan's management of the economy.

(*b*) *Foreign and defence policy*. Over half the voters approved of Reagan's handling of foreign affairs. The invasion of Grenada gave the President an immediate boost in popularity, but concerns were expressed on his nuclear weapon policy and over 60 per cent felt that the United States should do more

to reach agreement with the Soviet Union on arms proliferation.

Perhaps the most obvious explanation of Reagan's victory was
Reagan himself; his greatest strength was that even his opponents
liked him. His campaign managers focused on his 'image', not on
specific programmes. While Mondale stressed 'poverty, taxes and
gloom', concentrating on the increasing budget and trade deficits,
the President wrapped himself in the flag and spoke of a
'springtime of hope' and exuded optimism. Importantly, however,
to most voters he had delivered his promises, made in 1980, to
reduce inflation and unemployment and to make America strong
again. As Gerald Pomper had noted, Reagan may be 'a good
salesman, and his product may have been wrapped attractively,
even deceptively, but there was still a product'.

Reagan's victory in 1980 and his landslide in 1984 would make
it seem that the Democrats' position as the majority party was
doomed. The results of the 1986 mid-term elections, however,
make it clear that when it comes to congressional elections they
can beat the Republicans. Despite Reagan's campaigning on
behalf of GOP candidates, the electorate rejected this plea to vote
for him 'one more time'. In the Senate the Republicans defending
22 of the 34 seats fought last in the Reagan 1980 campaign lost 9
seats to the Democrats and gained one. Particularly galling for
GOP strategists were Democratic gains in the South, West and
Midwest where some had suggested a new Republican majority
was being born. The net result was a Democratic Senate majority
of 54–46. In the House the Democrats gained seven seats from the
Republicans, leaving them with a 260–175 margin.

Victory for the Democratic Party in the mid-term contests
suggested that the Reagan presidential wins in 1980 and 1984
were personal triumphs rather than a victory for the Republican
Party and that short-term forces were instrumental in providing
electoral majorities for him. The Democrats still retain their
majorities in both House of Congress and in most of the state
governments. But a closer examination of the division of the vote
in 1986 for Senate, House and gubernatorial (governorship) races
show only a 51 per cent–49 per cent Democratic plurality over the
Republicans. With the demographic changes taking place in the
electorate can a Republican plurality be far away?

Changes in the conduct of presidential election campaigns

In the last twenty-five years there have been many changes in the conduct of presidential election campaigns. Since 1960 there has been an increase in the number of primary elections; with the relative decline of political parties, aspiring presidential candidates have created their own personal campaign organisations; and finally, candidates, to get their political message across, have turned to television to reach the widest possible audience.

What effects have these changes in the conduct of campaigns had on the electorate?

The increase in presidential primaries

Presidential candidates are selected by their respective party conventions in the summer of each election year. Delegates attending that convention will have been chosen either at state conventions or at state primary elections held in the preceding months. Since 1968 the number of states holding primaries has risen dramatically from 17 to 30 in 1976 and 34 in 1980. The increase in the number of primaries meant that by 1980 almost 80 per cent of convention delegates were selected in this way. However, in 1984 the pattern changed. Firstly, the number of primaries fell to 26, while the number of states selecting delegates by the caucus system rose to 25 (these figures include the District of Columbia, which is not a state). Secondly, the time-span for delegate selection was reduced to 14 weeks, from 28 February, the date of the New Hampshire primary, to 5 June when primary elections took place in California and four other states. Within this period several states selected their delegates on the same day, for example 13 March became known as 'Fat Tuesday' as nine states selected 377 Democratic party delegates on that day. Finally, the Democrats changed the rules again for 1984, allowing 14 per cent of their delegates to the national convention in San Francisco to be selected from members of the House or Representatives and the Senate.

In 1988 the Democrats held primaries in 36 states, the Republicans primaries in 34 states as well as the District of Columbia and territories such as Puerto Rico. This year also saw the innovation of the regional primary – 'Super Tuesday' when 16 states (14 from the South) held primary elections on 8 March. This unprecedented concentration was the product of a strategy

devised by Southern Democrats, designed to promote the nomination of a moderate candidate electable in the South. Some 40
per cent of Democratic delegates and 33 per cent of Republican
delegates were selected on that day.

The larger number of primaries and the fact that, in most,
candidates are allocated delegates in proportion to their vote
(providing it is above 15 per cent) means that, if he is to be
successful in winning his party's nomination, he must contact
every primary and caucus to accumulate delegates. This in turn
means that each prospective candidate must build a personal
organisation to run their campaign, obtain adequate finance to
fund it and be prepared to be a full-time candidate for at least
three years before the election. The campaigns of Jimmy Carter in
1976, Ronald Reagan in 1980 (both unemployed ex-State Governors), and Walter Mondale in 1984 (an unemployed ex-Vice-
President), illustrate this. In 1988 George Bush had an advantage
as Republican Vice-President as he already had national standing
and time to campaign, as his primary job was hardly onerous.
Among the Democratic Party challengers Michael Dukakis,
Richard Gephardt, Albert Gore and Paul Simon were full-time
politicians while Bruce Babbitt, Jesse Jackson and Gary Hart
were free to campaign full time.

The second effect of the increase in the number of primaries has
been on the number of candidates who desire to run. In 1972 the
Democrats had 14 declared runners; in 1976, 12; 1984, 7; and
1988, 7. In 1980 the Republicans had 4 serious contenders and in
1988, 6. The Democrats have always had a larger field than
Republicans, mainly because they have a larger number of elected
politicians. For the voter, both primaries and caucuses are
divisive events which can undermine party loyalty as candidates,
seeking advantage, question colleagues' political credibility. Party
unity can be badly affected by a series of bitter intra-party
conflicts as, for example, the Ford–Reagan fight in 1976 and the
Carter–Kennedy battle in 1980.

Personal campaign organisation

Candidates seeking nomination for the presidency, of necessity,
have to create their own campaign organisation, or a party within
a party, to support their campaign. This organisation is essential
for a candidate to raise finance, plan his strategy for nomination
and election and plan media coverage. Again it is a divisive

activity: each candidate seeks resources – money, party workers and voters from within the totality of all his party's resources – and thus party member is set against party member. Often losing candidates show reluctance or are lukewarm in endorsing the eventual party nominee, as happened with Edward Kennedy in 1980 and Robert Dole in 1988.

The use of television

Television has become the medium through which political campaigns are conducted. Most voters do not experience political campaigns first-hand but follow them through television. In 1980, 76 per cent of the electorate named television as the most important source of campaign news. As well as television being the most important source of information, in the same year 56 per cent found it the most believable

Television has been widely used in presidential campaigns, from Nixon's 'Checkers' speech in 1952, in which he declared his innocence of corrupt election practices, to the Reagan–Mondale debates in 1984 and, increasingly, for political advertising.

By the late 1960s candidates were employing media consultants in their campaign staff for advice on presentation and particularly for political advertising, which is allowed in the United States. The 1984 election provides good examples of the types of political advertising. Political advertising can take two forms: negative and positive. A good example of 'negative' advertising, i.e., attacking one's opponent, was used by Walter Mondale against Gary Hart in the Democratic nomination contest. Mondale questioned Hart's alleged weak issue position by using a phrase from a popular hamburger advertisement. 'Where's the beef?' railed a diminutive old lady at the audience – implying that Hart's campaign lacked political substance. In 1988 George Bush's team made commercials attacking Dukakis's liberalism on prison furloughs, his patriotism on the pledge of allegiance and his record on coping with environmental pollution. In 1984 the Reagan campaign made a series of positive commercials, emphasising how strong America had become since 1980 in both economic and foreign policy. One commercial which portrayed the President and Nancy Reagan discussing their feelings for each other had a particular impact.

But what effect does television have on political campaigns? The major change concerns campaigning and traditional party functions. Candidate itineraries and speeches are planned to meet news deadlines and the campaign itself is now conducted primarily by media advisers, not party professionals.

The effect of media campaigns on the electorate is difficult to determine. The conventional wisdom is that the media select which candidates are to be considered seriously by the voters, favour the most telegenic and magnify mistakes. However, an analysis of recent elections challenges these views. In 1980 the charismatic Edward Kennedy was defeated by dull Jimmy Carter. In 1984 John Glenn had a massive media coverage with the release of *The Right Stuff* film, but finished sixth in the Iowa caucuses. A front runner can overcome a bad press, as did Reagan after an inadequate television debate with Walter Mondale in 1984. Finally, evidence from the 1988 election suggest that voters remember Bush's 'revolving door' commercial on prison furloughs equally with a Dukakis release which emphasised the family and education.

Certainly, a modern presidential campaign is dominated by television coverage with candidates scheduling appearances, delivering speeches in 'sound bites', and actively looking for television opportunities. Television has also made some important contributions to politics; regional differences have been narrowed and people are more knowledgeable about politics. But as David Broder has argued, its 'biggest effect on our politics has been to lessen the substance of the campaign itself'.

By focusing on some of the changes in the conduct of presidential election campaigns, we have attempted to show how the stability of the voting coalitions of both political parties can be threatened. Although primaries were designed to increase party members' participation in the selection process of presidential candidates, the actual contests themselves are divisive. Candidate campaign organisations, essential for a long primary campaign, spend resources on internecine warfare. Meanwhile, television provides the electorate with most of its political information, gradually acquiring what had been a central party function, and in so doing helping to weaken partisan attachments.

Conclusion

Changes in the way in which presidential elections are conducted, physical change in the electorate, the emergence of new issues and

candidates in politics, the decline in party voting and the increase
in split-ticket voting has led many political scientists to conclude
that the Democratic Party coalition put together by Franklin
Roosevelt in the 1930s is now slowly fragmenting. Certainly the
Republican Party has cause for optimism, winning five of the last
six presidential elections, but to date the GOP has been unable to
translate victories at the presidential level into majorities in both
Houses of Congress and in statewide elections. The Democrats
still remain the majority party in the United States, but how
tenuous is their grip on that position?

Further reading

W. H. Flanigan and N. H. Zingale, *Political Behaviour of the
American Electorate*, 5th edn, Allyn & Bacon Inc., 1983.

N. Nie *et al.*, *The Changing American Voter*, 2nd edn, Harvard
University Press, 1979.

M. P. Wattenberg, *The Decline of American Political Parties
1956–84*, Harvard University Press, 1986.

Questions

1. How important is party identification in determining the
vote of the individual elector?

2. What are the long- and short-term forces which affect
presidential elections?

12

THE 1988 ELECTIONS

Introduction

On 8 November 1988 George Herbert Walker Bush defeated Michael Dukakis by eight points in the popular vote and a 426–112 margin in the electoral college, to become the 41st President of the United States. In so doing, Bush earned a note in the history books by becoming the first Vice-President since Martin van Buren in 1836 to be elected to the presidency at the conclusion of his vice-presidential term.

The Bush victory, as already noted, the fifth Republican win since 1968, led many commentators to question whether the Democratic Party were still a force in presidential politics. Two victories each by Richard Nixon and Ronald Reagan and only one by Democrat Jimmy Carter, and that in arguably exceptional circumstances, have led to suggestions that there is a Republican electoral lock on the White House. Yet outside presidential contests the GOP does not fare so well. Apart from Republican control from 1980–86 the US Senate has had a Democratic Party majority in recent history. The House has been solidly Democratic since 1955 and after the mid-term elections in 1986 the party controlled 26 of the 50 state governorships. The election of Republican George Bush in 1988 with a Congress controlled by the Democratic Party tends to suggest that there may be an emerging Republican voting majority in support of GOP candidates for the White House, but a Democratic voting majority in elections for the House and Senate.

The structure of presidential election campaigns

Campaigns for the presidency can be divided into four main stages.

(*a*) *Pre-primary stage*. Immediately after each presidential election commentators begin to identify likely runners for the next contest. For example, in 1984 Governor Mario Cuomo was tipped as a strong runner for the Democrats along with George Bush and Robert Dole for the Republicans. During the three years prior to election year candidates begin to raise money, put together a campaign organisation, tour the country assessing support, and begin to raise their political profile. Personal candidate organisations are essential to meet the requirements of modern campaigning and time is needed to organise these.

(*b*) *Primary and caucus stage*. In the year of the election voters in each state select delegates for its national convention, which will pick the party presidential nominee. These delegates are chosen either in a presidential primary open to all registered party members, or by party caucus. In 1988 the Democrats held 36 primaries and the Republicans 34. Broadly, as each candidate will acquire delegates at each primary election in proportion to his vote, candidates are forced to run in as many primaries as resources and political support allow. In 1988 the primary/caucus season lasted from 16 February in New Hampshire to 14 June in North Dakota. This four-month campaign trail is arduous, expensive and tiring for candidates, but serves to shake down the personal campaign organisation of the winning candidate for the general election.

(*c*) *Party convention stage*. In recent years this has usually ratified the choice made in the primary/caucus stage, and crowns the party's presidential candidate. The convention also approves the party platform and endorses the candidate's choice of vice-presidential running mate. Conventions, too, provide a unifying function, bringing the party together after what has often been a divisive primary stage, and gives the first national platform for the winning candidate to begin his campaign for the presidency.

(*d*) *General election stage*. The general election campaign begins on Labor Day, the first Monday in September, and candidates will usually focus their attention on the nine states with the largest number of votes in the electoral college. The number of electoral college votes in the 'big nine' (the most popular) states totals 241 of the 270 needed to win the presidency. Campaign appearances are highly structured media events designed to make good television and will be timed to make the evening news bulletins. Since 1960, and the famous Kennedy–Nixon debates, a televised confrontation between the candidates has become a regular feature of the campaign. Finally, candidates will spend about two-thirds of their budget on advertising. In recent years 'negative' advertising has dominated, for example the famous Daisy Girl advertisement sponsored by Lyndon Johnson in 1964. Come election day candidates will have travelled thousands of miles, spent millions of dollars and worked themselves to the point of exhaustion for almost a year to win the race for the White House.

The 1988 presidential campaign

The Democrats: from Iowa to Atlanta

1. The candidates   By the beginning of 1988 the leading contenders for the Democratic Party nomination were Bruce Babbitt, former Governor of Arizona, Michael Dukakis, Governor of Massachusetts, Richard Gephardt, Congressman from Missouri, Albert Gore, Senator for Tennessee, Gary Hart, former Senator for Colorado, Jesse Jackson, former aide to Martin Luther King and Paul Simon, Senator from Illinois.

Missing from the list of contenders was Governor Mario Cuomo, who had been tipped in 1984 as the leading contender for 1988 and favoured by a majority of party supporters. His withdrawal on the grounds that the quest for the presidency would place unacceptable stresses on his family illustrates how demanding such a campaign can be. Gary Hart's re-entry into the race after a scandal forced him to retire in May 1987 made him the leading contender until the Iowa caucuses on 8 February.

2. The primary and caucus phase

(*a*) *The first phase: Iowa to New Hampshire.* Richard Gephardt emerged the winner of the Iowa caucuses with 31 per cent of the votes, followed by Paul Simon with 27 per cent and Dukakis, 22 per cent. Gephardt had spent some $0.5 million on television advertising, proclaiming his support for the adoption of trade barriers in a state where the farming community was going through a recession.

The New Hampshire primary was won by Dukakis, who had a 16 per cent lead over Gephardt, and Hart finished bottom of the

Table 12.1   Super Tuesday results – Democrats

	Votes cast	*% votes*
Jackson	2,589,784	26.7
Dukakis	2,568,260	26.5
Gore	2,488,905	25.6
Gephardt	1,236,195	12.7
Others	823,495	8.2

poll. Gephardt won South Dakota by 12 percentage points over Dukakis, but the latter was victorious in the Minnesota caucuses. The stresses of the campaign were being felt by Simon whose time was now divided between campaigning and fund-raising and he withdrew from the Super Tuesday contests. Jesse Jackson continued to attract support, winning 20 per cent of the Minnesota vote and polling well in some white areas. At the end of February Dukakis won in Maine and in Vermont, where Jackson polled 26 per cent of the vote.

(*b*) *Super Tuesday*. On 8 March, 16 states, 14 in the South, held primaries. This unprecedented concentration of primary activity was designed by southern Democrats to promote the nomination of a moderate Democratic candidate, electable in the South. The outcome was indecisive.

Jackson won 5 Deep South states, Gore a further 5, Dukakis 5 (Florida, Maryland, his home state Massachusetts, Rhode Island and Texas) and Gephardt one, his home state Missouri. Far from reducing the field, all candidates could claim victories:

(*i*) *Jesse Jackson* claimed 90 per cent of the black vote in 10 of the states, but only 10 per cent of the white vote.

(*ii*) *Albert Gore*, who spent $2 million and risked all on Super Tuesday to catapult him to the next phase, did better than expected and came second in 4 of the 5 states won by Jackson.

(*iii*) *Michael Dukakis* won, not unexpectedly, 2 in New England and the 2 most popular, Texas and Florida, plus Maryland, plus running respectably in the Old South.

(*iv*) *Richard Gephardt* who won, as expected, in Missouri, was the real loser who came a poor second in Oklahoma and third in Florida.

No front runner emerged as a result of Super Tuesday, contrary to expectations. The contest, if anything, enhanced the candidancy of Jackson, who was unacceptable to the Southern white Democratic establishment. Success was achieved in generating momentum and over 10 million voters participated in the Democratic primaries. Super Tuesday finally saw the withdrawal of Gary Hart, who failed to win a single delegate in any of the primaries.

(c) *The middle phase – Jackson* v. *Dukakis*. Following victory in the caucuses in South Carolina on 12 March, the campaign trail led north to Illinois, and the rustbelt. The result was a Simon victory in his home state, but with Jackson second and Dukakis a poor third, the nomination remained wide open. Jackson captured 91 per cent of the black vote (and only 9 per cent of the white), highlighting the narrow electoral base of his campaign. The Jackson momentum continued in the Michigan caucus on 26 March where he beat Dukakis into a poor second place, even though the latter had the support of Coleman Young, the black mayor of Detroit. With only 3 per cent of the voting-age population participating, Dukakis could claim the result was not that critical. But it does indicate, however, what the highly motivated Jackson campaign organisation could achieve, and the portents bode ill for the Dukakis camp which appeared unable to mobilise their vote. Illinois, too, claimed another casualty when Richard Gephardt announced he was abandoning the race.

With Jackson now in the ascendant, Dukakis needed a victory to sustain his momentum. This came in Connecticut on 29 March when he won 58 per cent of the vote to Jackson's 28 per cent. Dukakis also won in Wisconsin, beating Jackson into second place by 20 percentage points. Exit polls gave Dukakis 51 per cent of the vote to Jackson's 28 per cent. Dukakis also won in Wisconsin, beating Jackson into second place by 20 percentage points. Exit polls gave Dukakis 51 per cent of the white vote and 9 per cent of the black, while Jackson polled 88 per cent of the black and 23 per cent of the white vote.

At the beginning of April Paul Simon effectively withdrew from contention, suspending his campaign, while Dukakis, Jackson and Gore headed for New York and the most bitter primary of the campaign. Here Albert Gore, seeking to re-establish himself following Super Tuesday, attacked both Dukakis and Jackson. Spending over $1 million on television commercials aimed primarily at the Jewish vote, Gore berated Jackson for his alleged support of Yaser Arafat, the Palestine Liberation Organisation leader, and Fidel Castro – to no avail. Dukakis won over 50 per cent of the vote, Jackson came second with 37 per cent and Gore trailed third with 10 per cent. Polls revealed the collapse of the Gore strategy, Dukakis winning over 80 per cent of the Jewish vote, and so he withdrew. In Pennsylvania a week later Dukakis effectively clinched victory over Jackson, taking 67 per cent of the vote and 165 delegates to the convention.

(d) *Triumph in the West*. New York and Pennsylvania were the turning points in the primary contests. Although Jackson won in the District of Columbia, Dukakis took every other primary, winning the final four, including California, with 67 per cent of the vote on 7 June.

In the four months following the Iowa caucuses the almost unknown Dukakis had come from a third place in the Iowa caucuses to effectively win the Democratic Party nomination outright. In December 1987, some 74 per cent of the voting public had no idea who he was but by July he was leading George Bush in the polls by 17 percentage points. Although Jackson had control of the black vote, Dukakis had built an electoral constituency to possibly win the presidency. His campaign was well financed and organised; if he could unite the party at the convention in Atlanta, many Democrats felt he could beat the Republicans in November.

3. *The convention in Atlanta* Following the victory in California, Dukakis sought a running mate. He was perceived by most voters as a New England, interventionist liberal, and hence the choice of vice-presidential nominee was critical to balance the ticket. Poll data indicated that if Jackson were chosen, Democrats would lose, so the choice was restricted effectively to a conservative from the South or West. Throughout June and early July, Dukakis consulted with leading Democratic Party politicians, including defeated candidates Gore, Gephardt and Jackson. The latter certainly pressed a strong case commenting that 'others [candidates] under consideration are unknown quantities beyond their districts and beyond their home state', thus implying that he was not, and had a national constituency.

On 12 July, Dukakis announced that Senator Lloyd Bentsen from Texas would be his running mate. Undoubtedly Dukakis thought to rekindle the memories of the 1960 campaign when the Massachusetts–Texas team of Kennedy and Johnson defeated

Nixon and Lodge. The choice of conservative Bentsen was important. Dukakis sought to reassure white voters in the South who, in recent presidential elections, had abandoned the Democratic Party, and in addition he needed to convince the American people that he was not a big-spending liberal who would raise taxes and go soft on the Soviet Union. The choice of Bentsen angered Jackson supporters who felt their candidate had not been properly consulted. Their feelings were summarised by Ben Hooks, Director of the influential NAACP, who commented, 'Sometimes we support enthusiastically, sometimes we just support and sometimes we support with the brakes on.'

The highlights of what was a well-managed convention were the keynote address of Ann Richards who railed on Bush as the man born 'with a silver foot in his mouth' and a plea for unity by Jesse Jackson, who after meeting Dukakis to heal the rift between them over the choice of Bentsen, agreed not to put his name forward for the vice-presidential nomination.

The convention endorsed the Dukakis platform that committed the party to little that was unpopular, and the Governor duly crowned the party nominee for the presidency. In his acceptance speech he set what was to be the tone of his campaign declaring, 'if anyone tells you that the American dream belongs to the privileged few and not all of us, you tell them that the Reagan era is over ... and a new era is about to begin'.

On this high note, with 93 per cent of delegates believing that the Dukakis–Bentsen ticket could beat George Bush, and the Democratic Party candidate leading in the polls by 17 percentage points, party workers felt they had a good chance of winning the presidency for the first time since 1976.

The Republicans
1. The candidates In January 1988, apart from Vice-President George Bush, the leading Republican contender, the other candidates seeking the nomination were Robert Dole, Senator from Kansas and vice-presidential nominee in 1976; General Al Haig, former Reagan Secretary of State; Congressman Jack Kemp from New York, Pierre Du Pont, former Governor of Delaware and Pat Robertson, television evangelist.

Most commentators felt that the contest would be between Bush and Dole with the Vice-President emerging as the victor. Bush had all the advantages, eight years as Reagan's Vice-

President, name recognition in the electorate, a well-financed and organised campaign team. Pat Robertson was the unknown quantity. As a leading television evangelist, his constituency lay in the bible belt where with his band of evangelic Christians he presented himself as the true heir of Reagan conservatism.

2. The primary and caucus phase

(a) *The early rounds.* The first caucus in Michigan, bedevilled by bitter recriminations, set the tone of the Republican primary contests. Pat Robertson was expected to beat Bush (who had won there in 1980), lost to the Vice-President following a series of legal challenges and the desertion of his ally Jack Kemp, the other conservative Republican, to Bush. Dole won easily in his home state Kansas, but the real upset came when Bush lost to Dole in the Iowa caucuses, coming a poor third to Pat Robertson. The Bush defeat in Iowa, where he was expected to do well, set back his campaign. The Dole victory was particularly welcome, following angry exchanges in the Senate with the Vice-President over comments by Bush staff about the Dole family.

A Bush win in a bitter New Hampshire primary where he made use of explicit anti-Dole television advertisements put the Vice-President's campaign back on course. But the victory was soured by the withdrawal of Al Haig who publicly endorsed Robert Dole. Dole, however, did not enhance his reputation as a bad loser by commenting in defeat that he wished Bush 'would stop telling lies about me'.

In the remaining contests before Super Tuesday, Dole won decisively in the Minnesota caucus, taking 42.6 per cent of the vote and 55 per cent of the primary vote in South Dakota. Robertson came second and Bush third in both. The Dole bandwagon received a jolt with a Bush victory in the Vermont primary where he trailed the Vice-President by 10 per cent and in South Carolina on 5 March where Bush won with 48 per cent of the vote. By Super Tuesday Haig and Du Pont had withdrawn, leaving Bush and Dole locked in a bitter personal contest, as well as Pat Robertson who hoped to run well in his homeland, the bible belt.

(b) *Super Tuesday.* For George Bush Super Tuesday effectively gave him the Republican nomination. He won all fourteen of the Southern states and two in New England. He gained over 50 per cent of the vote in all but four states, and his well-financed campaign which had been working in the South for

Table 12.1 Super Tuesday results – Republican

	Votes cast	% votes
Bush	2,761,045	56.9
Dole	1,151,887	23.7
Robertson	624,814	12.9
Kemp	235,259	4.9
Others	80,379	1.7

months crushed Dole. In addition, in one day, he collected 574 delegates and created a momentum that would give him the Republican nomination in New Orleans

For Dole, Super Tuesday effectively marked the end of his campaign which was bedevilled by infighting and poor financial management. Senior staff were publicly sacked and the budget had overrun by 50 per cent before the campaign proper had begun: as a result advertising planned for Super Tuesday was cut by 60 per cent.

Super Tuesday, too, saw the end of the Robertson campaign. Despite hoping to do well in the bible belt, he was comprehensively beaten into a poor third place, winning only seven delegates. Poll data revealed that of the 39 per cent of Republican primary voters calling themelves born-again Christians, Bush captured more of their votes than Robertson.

Although Dole and Robertson were effectively out of the Republican race following Super Tuesday, only Jack Kemp formally withdrew, his attempt to capture the conservative wing of the party having failed. Paradoxically, Super Tuesday, which was designed by Southern Democrats to promote the nomination of a Democratic Party candidate, electable in the south, did just that for Republican George Bush.

(c) *Bush in the ascendant.* From Illinois through to California in June, George Bush staked his claim to the nomination. In Illinois on 15 March he beat Dole, taking 55 per cent of the primary vote to the latter's 36 per cent. In Connecticut the Vice-President won 70.6 per cent on 29 March and that evening Dole formally withdrew, promising in the interests of party unity to support George Bush. Robertson remained in the race, but in name only. The Republican primaries and caucuses had selected George Bush to succeed Ronald Reagan.

3. From California to New Orleans Between the California primary and the Republican Party convention in New Orleans the Vice-President began to plan his strategy to win the presidency. In June and July 1988 the Reagan legacy was not so attractive as a year before. Revelations about the corruption in the Reagan administration, the 'sleaze factor', were emerging. A special prosecutor's investigation into Attorney-General Ed Meese's role in an aborted $1 million Iraqi pipeline deal, resignations in the Justice Department, fraud investigations in the Pentagon and the Iran–Contra affair, all threatened to undermine the Bush candidacy. In addition, Bush was trailing Dukakis in the polls by 17 percentage points after the Atlanta convention.

To establish himself as a candidate in his own right, and not a Reagan puppet, Bush, in the months before New Orleans, began to quietly dissassociate himself from some aspects of the administration.

(*a*) In a series of highly publicised speeches he attempted to widen his electoral base. Addressing a Cuban immigrant gathering, he promised no *rapprochement* with the Castro government. He promised to appoint an Hispanic to his Cabinet if elected, and to appeal to women voters he appointed Sheila Tate as his chief press adviser. To the NAACP he spoke of improvements he wished to make on the civil rights enforcement, distancing himself from the Reagan record.

(*b*) *The use of incumbency*. Bush used the vice-presidency to promote his candidacy, particularly following the shooting-down by a US destroyer of an Iranian airbus in the Persian Gulf. In an unprecedented appearance, for a Vice-President, at the United Nations he put the American case, creating the impression that, unlike Dukakis, he was experienced in the handling of foreign affairs and crisis decision-making.

(*c*) *Presidential endorsements*. Although Bush wanted to distance himself from problems in the Reagan administration, the President was still personally very popular, and a personal endorsement from the President would help his campaign. In an emotional speech at the convention Ronald Reagan told the audience, 'George, I'm in your corner', and said that he would leave his 'phone number and address behind just in case you need a foot soldier', while promising to campaign actively for the ticket. Inadvertently perhaps, the President also set the tone for what became a bitter campaign. Addressing the nation he commented, 'You'll never hear that "L" word liberal from them . . . [the Democrats] have slipped their platform into a brown wrapper', intimating that the Democratic party were trying to mislead the electorate. The 'liberalism' theme would be an issue that the Bush campaign developed in the autumn.

4. The convention in New Orleans   The Republican convention, following the farewell appearance of the retiring President, was a dull and businesslike affair. It endorsed a bland 104-page platform entitled 'An American vision – for our children and our future', pledging the continuation of the Reagan agenda: no tax increases, support for the Strategic Defense Initiative and a constitutional amendment banning abortion.

One problem remained, who would be the vice-presidential nominee? In July, a poll of Republican activists showed over 20 per cent supporting Bob Dole: others favoured Jack Kemp. Elizabeth Dole (the Senator's wife and former Transportation Secretary) and former Senator Howard Baker were contenders. The choice of Dan Quayle surprised everybody. Like Dukakis, Bush sought to balance the ticket to enchance this electoral appeal. Senator Quayle represented the Reagan wing of the party – he opposed abortion, distrusted the USSR, favoured Star Wars and school prayers. He was also young (41 against Bush's 64) and from the Midwestern state of Indiana. In selecting Quayle, Bush sent a message to conservative Republicans, who thought him weak, that he was one of them.

In his acceptance speech Bush rallied the party faithful, declaring that although he was the underdog he meant 'to run hard, to stand on the issues – and I mean to win'.

The Dukakis 17 percentage point lead in August, Lee Atwater, the Bush chief of staff noted, was a temporary phenomenon, 'No matter what the polls look like this is going to be a close election.' A brave prediction, when days after the convention the Bush judgement was questioned on his selection of Dan Quayle who, it was revealed, pulled strings to avoid the draft in 1968 which could have sent him to Vietnam.

The general election
Although the election campaign began in September, for the Bush campaign organisation the starting date was 26 May 1988. In

Paramus, New Jersey, five aides led by Lee Atwater were watching thirty Democratic swing voters who had voted for Reagan in 1984 being tested for their reaction to some negative commercials about Michael Dukakis. These guinea pigs were told about the Massachusetts prison-release system which had allowed a convicted murderer to commit rape while on parole; about Dukakis vetoing a bill requiring teachers to lead their classes in the pledge of allegiance and about pollution in Boston harbour. By the end of the evening fifteen of the group had switched sides, allowing Atwater to comment 'that the sky was the limit on the Dukakis negatives'. This meeting set the strategy of the Bush campaign.

The Democrats, meanwhile, after the convention just relaxed. The Dukakis campaign organisation, having won the nomination, failed to develop a strategy to win the general election. Dukakis thought that the promise of good jobs and effective government – the Massachusetts model – could be translated to the national political arena. Leading Democrats, too, may have been complacent about their lead in the polls, and the fact that many believed that the Vice-President would be blamed for the problems of the Reagan administration, the Iran–Contra affair, the budget deficit, and the Bush connection with General Noriega of Panama. On the other hand, the Democratic Party was united behind Dukakis and there was little of the intra-party conflict that had been present in the presidential elections of 1968, 1972 and 1980. How then could Dukakis lose?

The simple explanation is that Dukakis allowed the Vice-President to set the agenda. Bush made no specific policy pledges: he promised no new taxes, a flexible freeze to reduce the budget deficit and a 'kinder, gentler' American. Instead he fought a negative campaign attacking Dukakis on four points.

(*a*) Dukakis's softness on crime, brought graphically to the screen with the prison furlough advertisements. Bush also took several opportunities to appear on prime-time television surrounded by policemen where he spoke on the law and order issues.

(*b*) His lack of patriotism, again through advertisements, but also by Bush reciting the pledge of allegiance before every meeting.

(*c*) His liberalism – Bush intimating that this was an un-

American philosophy associated with high-spending centralised governments. Bush by contrast emphasised his
conservative values as being in the mainstream of American
throught.

(d) His record on pollution in Boston Harbour. Bush was
filmed fishing garbage from the waterfront.

Even the presidential debates where Dukakis was expected to
shine, Bush set the agenda. The Vice-President agreed to two,
when Dukakis wanted four, timing them to end three weeks
before the election so that mistakes might be overcome. In the
event the only major error emerged in the vice-presidential
debates when Dan Quayle, claiming he had as much experience as
John Kennedy when he ran for the presidency in 1960, earned the
reproof from Lloyd Bentsen: 'I served with Jack Kennedy, Jack
Kennedy was a friend of mine. Senator, you're no Jack Kennedy'
– to which Quayle had no response.

The success of the Bush strategy is evident in the opinion poll
data. In mid-September the candidates were neck and neck, but
by October and the first debate Bush was 5–6 points ahead. By the
end of the month a Bush victory was predicted as he pulled into a
10–15 point lead.

With nothing to lose, Dukakis, in the final weeks of the
campaign, counter-attacked. He began to appeal to the traditional Democratic Party voting coalition, the blue-collar workers,
that he was the true inheritor of the party tradition. He spoke of
his belief in welfare state liberalism and attacked the get-rich-
quick attitudes of the Reagan administration. To many his
challenge came too late and on election day he was still trailing in
the polls.

Interpreting the presidential election

The night before the election both parties spent several million
dollars buying half-hour advertising slots to get their final
messages across. Dukakis tried to appeal to the head, discussing
issues including those raised in the Bush commercials, while Bush
appealed to the heart, focusing on family values and the pledge of
allegiance. But the general tenor of the campaign so dominated by
negative advertising and of charge and counter-charge, it is not
surprising that the turn-out on election day was a little over 50 per
cent of registered voters.

As had been predicted, George Bush won with 54 per cent of
those who voted to Mike Dukakis's 46 per cent. The result was no
landslide for Bush, who was victorious in 40 states taking 426
electoral college votes, against majorities in 10 states and the
District of Columbia for Dukakis who won 112. Dukakis polled
better than any Democratic presidential candidate, except Jimmy
Carter, since 1964 (see page 150). He also won New York and
Wisconsin, which had voted for Reagan in 1980 and 1984, as well
as gaining Washington, Oregon, with Iowa voting for a
Democratic candidate for the first time since 1972.

An analysis of the results on a state-by-state basis supports
both Lee Atwater's comment in the summer that the Republicans
had a solid 210 electoral college votes before the campaign began,
but also the view that there is no consequent Republican electoral
lock on the White House. In 15 states, mainly in the South and
West, Bush polled over 60 per cent of the vote, acquiring 107
electoral college votes and a further 15 between 55–60 per cent
with 174. But in 10 states, including California, Illinois and
Pennsylvannia, Bush was no more than 6 percentage points ahead
of Dukakis. Perhaps there is a glimmer of hope here for the
Democrats.

The regional pattern does illustrate how the parties have
changed places. The Democrats have lost, at least at the
presidential level, their Southern constituency. Bush dominated
the confederate states, running 22 percentage points ahead in
Florida, an average of 20 in the Deep South and 16 in the Upper
South. The South is now a Republican stronghold in presidential
elections. Although Dukakis polled well in the industrial states,
he only won New York, Massachusetts and West Virginia. His
victories in Minnesota and Wisconsin could be put down to the
agricultural depression, low prices and surplus production in the
1980s.

The inability of the Democrats to win in the South was driven
home in Texas, where the Bush–Quayle ticket polled 57 per cent
of the vote, but Lloyd Bentsen retained his Senate seat by a
comfortable margin.

Social-group voting patterns
In 1980 and 1984 Reagan victories seriously undermined the
traditional Democratic Party socio-economic voting coalition.
But in 1988 the Democrats could take some comfort, as Table

Table 12.3 Presidential vote by social group 1980–88

| | Vote in 1980[a] | | Vote in 1984 | | Vote in 1988 | |
	Reagan	Carter	Reagan	Mondale	Bush	Dukakis
Total	51	41	59	40	53	45
Men	55	36	62	37	57	41
Women	47	45	56	44	50	49
White	55	36	64	35	59	40
Black	11	85	9	89	12	86
Hispanic	35	56	37	61	30	69
18–29 yrs	43	44	59	40	52	47
30–44 yrs	54	36	57	42	54	45
45–59 yrs	55	39	59	39	57	42
60+	54	41	60	39	50	49
East	47	42	52	47	50	49
Midwest	51	40	58	40	52	47
South	52	44	64	36	58	41
West	53	34	61	38	52	46

Note: [a]Excluding vote for Anderson.
Source: New York Times/CBS News Exit Polls.

12.3 illustrates. The exit polls showed the electorate splitting along predictable demographic lines. On average the rich voted for Bush, the poor for Dukakis. The gender gap continued with Bush leading Dukakis among male voters by 16 percentage points while the women's vote was evenly divided. Dukakis had a 74 point majority among black voters and a 39 point lead among Hispanic speakers, but only won 40 per cent of the white vote. Generally Bush ran behind Reagan among all age groups. The over-60s divided almost evenly between both candidates, while in the 18–29 year old group Bush led by only 5 percentage points to Reagan's 19 in 1984. Perhaps most significantly, Dukakis attracted back into the party many of the Reagan Democrats. On this evidence George Bush was not able to consolidate the coalition assembled by Reagan in 1980 and 1984.

Explaining the Bush victory–party realignment?
1. Long-term influences Some commentators have suggested that the major effect of the Reagan presidency had been to create

the momentum for an enduring party realignment, the Republicans replacing the Democrats as the majority party. Does a third successive Republican presidential victory suggest any further evidence to support this view.

Poll data collected since 1980 reveals there has been no significant long-term shift in party allegiance among the electorate. In 1981 when Reagan became President 26 per cent considered themselves Republican and 37 per cent Democratic Party identifiers. Although Republican partisanship increased in 1984 (see Chapter 11), by the end of the Reagan administration in 1988 there had been minimal change, 28 per cent Republican and 38 per cent Democratic identifiers. If there was no *long-term* shift in partisanship from the Democratic to the Republican party, do short-term factors offer an explanation?

2. Short-term influences   Evidence that economic factors were influential in explaining the Bush victory abound. In 1984 Reagan posed the electorate a question. He asked whether most Americans felt 'better off today than they were in 1980'. Some 45 per cent of respondents replied they were better off and 30 per cent at the same level. Of these groups some 80 per cent voted for Reagan, indicating approval at his handling of the economy. In 1988, 60 per cent of the voters thought the economy was in better shape than in 1980, while 80 per cent felt their personal financial circumstances were very or fairly good. As in 1984, in 1988 75 per cent of those who thought the economy was improving voted for Bush while 66 per cent who felt it was deteriorating supported Dukakis. As in 1984 voters also felt the Republicans could manage the economy better than the Democrats, the former enjoying a 27 point lead.

This data reflects the success of the Reagan administration in managing the economy, as Table 12.4 indicates, every economic indicator showing improvement; inflation, unemployment and interest rates were down and the Bush victory can be in part explained by this phenomenon.

Despite this the public did indicate some concern on the budget and trade deficits, and 36 per cent thought that Bush should make balancing the budget his highest priority. Other issues hardly featured in the election: only 7 per cent rated defence spending, critical despite the high-profile Bush advertising campaign attac-

Table 12.4   Economic indicators 1980–88

	1980 (%)	1988 (%)
Inflation	12.5	4.2
Interest rates	15.5	10.0
Unemployment	7.5	5.2

king Dukakis.

As well as criticism of Dukakis's handling of the Massachusetts prison-release programme, Bush recited the pledge of allegiance or spoke of family values in campaign apperances. The Vice-President appeared surrounded by tough-looking policemen, yet less than 2 per cent of the electorate thought these issues important enough to affect their vote. In contrast, 31 per cent felt economic issues to be the most important, to 19 per cent social issues and 16 per cent foreign and defence matters were the most important issues.

The campaign commercials may not have *set the agenda* for the election but they did have an impact on voters' perceptions of each candidate. Bush was perceived to be tougher on crime, more patriotic and the more conservative of the two candidates, and his negative advertising certainly helped to sharpen this image. Dukakis seen as the more liberal, weak on law and order and foreign and defence issues – the reverse image of Bush. But in the last analysis it was bread-and-butter issues, the electorate's satisfaction with the Republican management of the economy and their reluctance to change this, which gave Bush the key to the White House.

The congressional and gubernatorial elections

Although most attention is focused on the race for the White House, equally important election contests were taking place across the nation in November, which in their own way will have an effect on the political climate in the next four years. Despite a convincing victory in the presidential election, the Bush coat-tails proved too short to carry many fellow Republicans in the Senate, House and gubernatorial races. Following the pattern of recent years, voters were quite happy to split their ticket, electing a

Republican to the White House and Democrats to control Congress.

The Senate

In the Senate, 33 seats were contested, but only 15 were in Republican control. Democratic Party strategists expected to retain control of the upper chamber, and in the event made a net gain of 1 seat.

The Republicans lost 4 seats, incumbents being defeated in Connecticut, where long-standing liberal Lowell Weiker was defeated, Nebraska and Nevada, and in an open contest in Virginia where former Govenor Charles Robb (Democrat) won by a landslide. The GOP could take some consolation, defeating a Democrat incumbent in Montana and winning open seats in Florida and Mississippi, strengthening their political hold in the South.

If 'liberalism' played a role in the presidential elections, in the Senate contests, ideology was not a death blow to senatorial ambition. Ohio liberal Republican Howard Metzenbaum (Republican), held his seat comfortably, defeating a conservative Democrat in a state which Bush carried by 10 percentage points.

The slight strengthening of Democratic Party control in the Senate guarantees that President Bush will not enjoy much of a honeymoon in dealing with Congress. Some Republican leaders felt that their presidential candidate could have campaigned more for party candidates. Some Senate results were very close, the Republicans only winning Florida after a recount, where Bush won by 22 percentage points.

The House of Representatives

In the House, the Democrats made a net gain of three seats giving them a 260–175 majority. Of the 408 incumbents who were running for re-election, only 6 lost. Their defeats in most cases due to scandals surrounding their ethical conduct. One case of note was that of Pat Swindall (Republican) who was charged with perjury in a case involving money laundering. He was defeated by Ben Jones, who once played a character in the 'Dukes of Hazzard' television show.

Performance in House elections is explained in large part by the power of incumbency where the advantages of free mailing and press attention, an organisational base in the district and campaign finance make them likely winners.

State governors

Both parties can take some comfort from the results of the 12 governorship races. The Democrats celebrated a net gain of one governor giving them a 28–22 edge nationally, the Republicans could be relieved at not losing more.

At the start of the campaign, the Democrats had hoped to win as many as 3 or 4 of the 8 Republican governerships up for election. In the event the Democrats took Republican seats in Indiana and West Virginia, losing in Montana. The Democrats' biggest consolation came in Indiana (the home of Dan Quayle) where Evan Bayh, the son of former US Senator Birch Bayh (who lost his seat to Quayle in 1980), became the state's first Democratic governor for twenty years and enjoyed perhaps a little family revenge.

Victory in the gubernatorial races is important because state governors will oversee the strategically important re-districting which will take place after the national census in 1990.

Evidence from the Senate, House and gubernatorial elections suggests that there is no long-term realignment towards the Republicans. Unlike the Reagan election of 1980, there was no great Republican coat-tails effect. Perhaps voters now are more sophisticated: Republicans are preferred to run national affairs, the Democrats to be the ombudsmen, the custodians of the local interests. A more persuasive explanation perhaps is that the electoral process has become fragmented and individualistic and the resources given to candidates and not parties mean that incumbents have advantages over challengers and, as 1988 showed, in all elections are likely to be victorious.

Towards 1992

The question remains, can the Democratic Party find a candidate to win a presidential election? Certainly there is no Republican electoral lock on the White House and the Bush victory in 1988 cannot be called a landslide. But with the Republicans now the presidential party in the South and West, broadly the sunbelt states, and with redistribution favouring them in 1992, the Democrats will find it harder still to win.

Survey data does offer some consolation for the Democrats. In terms of long-term party allegiance, some 38 per cent identify with the party of Roosevelt, Truman and Kennedy and there is no great increase in the number of Republican identifiers. If anything the United States is witnessing party *de-alignment*, with party attachments getting weaker and most voters considering themselves independents.

Even before election day Democratic presidential contenders for 1992 were laying their groundwork. Candidates currently include Jesse Jackson, Senator Bill Bradly of New Jersey, Senator Albert Gore, Governor Bill Clinton of Arkansas, Governor Mario Cuomo of New York and Senator Sam Nunn of Georgia. No matter who the Democrats chose, George Bush, the incumbent, will be the likely Republican candidate. It remains to be seen whether he follows in the footsteps of Martin van Buren who, after succeeding Andrew Jackson, served only one term, being defeated in 1840 by William Harrison. This was a defeat, historians claim, caused by the economic crisis of 1837. Will the budget and trade deficits be the undoing of President Bush and lead to a Democratic victory in 1992?

Questions

1. Why did the Republicans win the presidency in 1988?

2. From the evidence available in 1988 are the Republicans emerging as the new majority party?

THE CONSTITUTION OF THE UNITED STATES OF AMERICA

We the people of the United States, in order to form a more perfect Union, establish Justice, insure domestic Tranquility, provide for the common defence, promote the general Welfare, and secure the Blessing of Liberty to ourselves and our Posterity, do ordain and establish this CONSTITUTION for the United States of America.

Article I

Section 1. All legislative Powers herein granted shall be vested in a Congress of the United States, which shall consist of a Senate and House of Representatives. *Section 2.* The House of Representatives shall be composed of Members chosen every second Year by the People of the several States, and the Electors in each State shall have the Qualifications requisite for Electors of the most numerous Branch of the State Legislature.

No Person shall be a Representative who shall not have attained the Age of twenty-five Years, and been seven Years a Citizen of the United States, and who shall not, when elected, be an Inhabitant of that State in which he shall be chosen.

[Representatives and direct Taxes shall be apportioned among the several States which may be included within this Union, according to their respective Numbers, which shall be determined by adding to the whole Number of free Persons, including those bound to Service for a Term of Years, and excluding Indians not taxed, three-fifths of all other persons.][1] The actual Enumeration shall be made within three Years after the first Meeting of

---

[1] This provision was modified by the Sixteenth Amendment. The three-fifths reference to slaves was rendered obsolete by the Thirteenth and Fourteenth Amendments.

the Congress of the United States, and within every subsequent Term of ten Years, in such Manner as they shall be Law direct. The Number of Representatives shall not exceed one for every thirty thousand, but each State shall have at Least one Representative; and until such enumeration shall be made, the State of New Hampshire shall be entitled to chuse three, Massachusetts eight, Rhode Island and Providence Plantations one, Connecticut five, New York six, New Jersey four, Pennsylvania eight, Delaware one, Maryland six, Virginia ten, North Carolina five, South Carolina five, and Georgia three.

When vacancies happen in the Representation from any State, the Executive Authority thereof shall issue Writs of Election to fill such Vacancies.

The House of Representatives shall chuse their Speaker and other Officers; and shall have the sole Power of Impeachment.

Section 3. The Senate of the United States shall be composed of two Senators from each State, chosen by the Legislature thereof,[1] for six Years; and each Senator shall have one Vote.

Immediately after they shall be assembled in Consequence of the first Election, they shall be divided as equally as may be into three Classes. The Seats of the Senators of the first Class shall be vacated at the Expiration of the second Year, of the Second Class at the Expiration of the fourth Year, and the third class at the Expiration of the sixth Year, so that one-third may be chosen every second Year; and if Vacancies happen by Resignation, or otherwise, during the Recess of the Legislature of any State, the Executive thereof may make temporary Appointments until the next Meeting of the Legislature, which shall then fill such Vacancies.

No Person shall be a Senator who shall not have attained to the Age of thirty Years, and been nine Years a Citizen of the United States, and who shall not, when elected, be an Inhabitant of that State for which he shall be chosen.

The Vice President of the United States shall be President of the Senate, but shall have no Vote, unless they be equally divided.

The Senate shall chuse their other Officers, and also a President pro tempore, in the absence of the Vice President, or when he shall exercise the Office of President of the United States.

The Senate shall have the sole Power to try all Impeachments.

---

[1] See the Seventeenth Amendment.

When sitting for that Purpose, they shall be on Oath or Affirmation. When the President of the United States is tried, the Chief Justice shall preside; And no Person shall be convicted without the Concurrence of two-thirds of the Members present.

Judgment in Cases of Impeachment shall not extend further than to removal from Office, and disqualification to hold and enjoy any Office of honor, Trust or Profit under the United States; but the Party convicted shall nevertheless be liable and subject to Indictment, Trial, Judgment and Punishment, according to Law.

Section 4. The Times, Places and Manner of holding Elections for Senators and Representatives, shall be prescribed in each State by the Legislature thereof; but the Congress may at any time by Law make or alter such Regulations, except as to the Places of chusing Senators.

The Congress shall assemble at least once in every Year, and such Meeting shall be on the first Monday in December, unless they shall by Law appoint a different Day.[1]

Section 5. Each House shall be the Judge of the Elections, Returns and Qualifications of its own Members, and a Majority of each shall constitute a Quorum to do Business; but a smaller Number may adjourn from day to day, and may be authorized to compel the Attendance of absent Members, in such Manner, and under such Penalties as each House may provide.

Each House may determine the Rules of its Proceedings, punish its Members for disorderly Behavior, and, with the Concurrence of two-thirds, expel a Member.

Each House shall keep a Journal of its Proceedings and from time to time publish the same, excepting such Parts as may in their Judgment require Secrecy; and the Yeas and Nays of the Members of either House on any question shall, at the Desire of one-fifth of those Present, be entered on the Journal.

Neither House, during the Session of Congress, shall without the Consent of the other, adjourn for more than three days, nor to any other Place than that in which the two Houses shall be sitting.

Section 6. The Senators and Representatives shall receive a Compensation for their Services, to be ascertained by Law, and paid out of the Treasury of the United States. They shall in all Cases, except Treason, Felony, and Breach of the peace, be

[1] See the Twentieth Amendment.

privileged from Arrest during their Attendance at the Session of their respective Houses, and in going to and returning from the same; and for any Speech or Debate in either House, they shall not be questioned in any other Place.

No Senator or Representative shall, during the Time for which he was elected, be appointed to any civil Office under the Authority of the United States, which shall have been created, or the Emoluments whereof shall have been encreased during such time; and no Person holding any Office under the United States, shall be a Member of either House during his Continuance in Office.

Section 7. All Bills for raising Revenue shall originate in the House of Representatives; but the Senate may propose or concur with Amendments as on other Bills.

Every Bill which shall have passed the House of Representatives and the Senate, shall, before it become a Law, be presented to the President of the United States; If he approve he shall sign it, but if not he shall return it, with his Objections to that House in which it shall have originated, who shall enter the at large on their Journal, and proceed to reconsider it. If after such Reconsideration two-thirds of that House shall agree to pass the Bill it shall be sent, together with the Objections, to the other House, by which it shall likewise be reconsidered, and if approved by two-thirds of that House, it shall become a Law. But in all such Cases the Votes of both Houses shall be determined by Yeas and Nays, and the Names of the Persons voting to and against the Bill shall be entered on the Journal of each House respectively. If any Bill shall not be returned by the President within ten Days (Sunday excepted) after it shall have been presented to him, the Same shall be a Law, in like Manner as if he had signed it, unless the Congress by their Adjournment prevent its Return, in which Case it shall not be a Law.

Every Order, Resolution, or Vote to which the Concurrence of the Senate and House of Representatives may be necessary (except on a question of Adjournment) shall be presented to the President of the United States: and before the Same shall take Effect, shall be approved by him, or being disapproved by him, shall be repassed by two-thirds of the Senate and House of Representatives, according to the Rule and Limitations prescribed in the Case of a Bill.

Section 8. The Congress shall have Power To lay and collect

Taxes, Duties, Imposts and Excises, to pay the Debts and provide for the common Defence and general Welfare of the United States; but all Duties, Imposts and Excises shall be uniform throughout the United States;

To borrow money on the Credit of the United States;

To regulate Commerce with foreign Nations, and among the several States, and with the Indian Tribes;

To establish an uniform Rule of Naturalization, and uniform Laws on the subject of Bankruptcies throughout the United States.

To coin Money, regulate the Value thereof, and of foreign Coin, and fix the Standard of Weights and Measures;

To provide for the Punishment of counterfeiting the Securities and current Coin of the United States;

To establish Post Offices and post Roads;

To promote the Progress of Science and useful arts, by securing for limited Times to Authors and Inventors the exclusive Right to their respective Writings and Discoveries;

To constitute Tribunals inferior to the supreme Court;

To define and punish Piracies and Felonies committed on the high Seas, and Offenses against the Law of Nations;

To declare War, grant Letters of Marque and Reprisal, and make Rules concerning Captures on Land and Water;

To raise and support Armies, but no Appropriation of Money to that Use shall be for a longer Term than two Years;

To provide and maintain a Navy;

To make Rules for the Government and Regulation of the land and naval Forces;

To provide for calling forth the Militia to execute the Laws of the Union, suppress Insurrections and repel Invasions;

To provide for organizing, arming, and disciplining the Militia, and for governing such Part of them as may be employed in the Service of the United States, reserving to the States respectively, the Appointment of the Officers, and the Authority of training the Militia according to the discipline prescribed by Congress;

To exercise exclusive Legislation in all Cases whatsoever, over such District (not exceeding ten Miles square) as may, by Cession of particular States, and the acceptance of Congress become the Seat of the Government of the United States, and to exercise like Authority over all Places purchased by the Consent of the Legislature of the State in which the Same shall be, for the

Erection of Forts, Magazines, Arsenals, dock-Yards, and other needful Buildings;–And

To make all Laws which shall be necessary and proper for carrying into Execution the foregoing Powers, and all other Powers vested by this Constitution in the Government of the United States, or in any Department or Office thereof.

Section 9.   The Migration or Importation of such Persons as any of the States now existing shall think proper to admit, shall not be prohibited by the Congress prior to the Year one thousand eight hundred and eight, but a tax or duty may be imposed on such importation, not exceeding ten dollars for each Person.

The privilege of the Writ of Habeas Corpus shall not be suspended, unless when in Cases of Rebellion or Invasion the public Safety may require it.

No Bill of Attainder or ex post facto Law shall be passed.

No capitation, or other direct Tax shall be laid, unless in Proportion to the Census or Enumeration herein before directed to be taken.[1]

No Tax or Duty shall be laid on Articles exported from any State.

No Preference shall be given by an Regulation of Commerce or Revenue to the Ports of one State over those of another; nor shall Vessels bound to, or from one State, be obliged to enter, clear, or pay Duties in another.

No Money shall be drawn from the Treasury, but in Consequence of Appropriations made by Law; and a regular Statement and Account of the Receipts and Expenditures of all public Money shall be published from time to time.

No Title of Nobility shall be granted by the United States: And no Person holding any Office of Profit or Trust under them, shall, without the Consent of the Congress, accept of any present, Emolument, Office, or Title, of any kind whatever, from any King, Prince, or foreign State.

Section 10.   No State shall enter into any Treaty, Alliance, or Confederation; grant Letters of Marque and Reprisal; coin Money; emit Bills of Credit; make any Thing but gold and silver Coin a Tender in Payment of Debts; pass any Bill of Attainder, ex post facto Law, or Law impairing the Obligation of Contracts, or grant any Title of Nobility.

---

[1] See the Sixteenth Amendment.

No State shall, without the Consent of the Congress, lay any Imposts or Duties on Imports or Exports, except what may be absolutely necessary for executing its inspection Laws: and the net Product of all Duties and Imposts, laid by any State on Imports or Exports, shall be for the Use of the Treasury of the United States and all such Laws shall be subject to the Revision and Controul of the Congress.

No State shall, without the Consent of Congress, lay any duty of Tonnage, keep Troops, or Ships of War in time of Peace, enter into any Agreement or Compact with another State, or with a foreign Power, or engage in War, unless actually invaded, or in such imminent Danger as will not admit of delay.

ARTICLE II

Section 1. The executive Power shall be vested in a President of the United States of America. He shall hold his Office during the Term of four Years, and, together with the Vice President, chosen for the same Term, be elected, as follows

Each State shall appoint, in such Manner as the Legislature thereof may direct, a Number of Electors, equal to the whole number of Senators and Representatives to which the State may be entitled in the Congress; but no Senator or Representative, or Person holding an Office of Trust or Profit under the United States shall be appointed an Elector.

The Electors shall meet in their respective States, and vote by Ballot for two persons, of whom one at least shall not be an Inhabitant of the same State with themselves. And they shall make a List of all Persons voted for, and of the Number of Votes for each; which List they shall sign and certify, and transmit sealed to the Seat of the Government of the United States, directed to the President of the Senate. The President of the Senate shall, in the Presence of the Senate and House of Representatives, open all the Certificates, and the Votes shall then be counted. The Person having the greatest Number of Votes shall be the President, if such Number be a Majority of the whole Number of Electors appointed; and if there be more than one who have such Majority, and have an Equal Number of Votes, then the House of Representatives shall immediately chuse by Ballot one of them for President; and if no Person have a Majority, then from the five highest on the List the said House shall in like

Manner chuse the President, but in chusing the President, the Votes shall be taken by States, the Representation from each State having one Vote; A quorum for this Purpose shall consist of a Member or Members from two-thirds of the States, and a Majority of all the States shall be necessary to a Choice. In every Case, after the Choice of the President, the Person having the greatest Number of Votes of the Electors shall be the Vice-President. But if there should remain two or more who have equal votes, the Senate shall chuse from them by Ballot the Vice President.[1]

The Congress may determine the Time of chusing the Electors, and the Day on which they shall give their Vote; which Day shall be the same throughout the United States.

No person except a natural born Citizen, or a Citizen of the United States, at the time of the Adoption of this Constitution, shall be eligible to the Office of President; neither shall any Person be eligible to that Office who shall not have attained the Age of thirty-five Years, and been fourteen Years a Resident within the United States.

In Case of the Removal of the President from Office, or of his Death, Resignation, or Inability to discharge the Powers and Duties of the said office, the same shall devolve on the Vice President, and the congress may by Law provide for the Case of Removal, Death, Resignation or Inability, both the President and Vice President, declaring what Officer shall then act as President, and such Officer shall act accordingly, until the Disability be removed, or a President shall be elected.

The President shall, at stated Times, receive for his Services, a Compensation, which shall neither be encreased nor diminished during the Period for which he shall have been elected, and he shall not receive within that Period any other Emolument from the United States, or any of them.

Before he enters on the Execution of his Office, he shall take the following Oath or Affirmation:–"I do solemnly swear (or affirm) that I will faithfully execute the Office of President of the United States, and will to the best of my Ability, preserve, protect and defend the Constitution of the United States."

Section 2.   The President shall be Commander in Chief of the Army and Navy of the United States, and of the Militia of the

---

[1]   This paragraph was superseded by the Twelfth Amendment.

several States, when called into the actual Service of the United States; he may require the Opinion in writing, of the principal officer in each of the executive Departments, upon any subject relating to the Duties of their respective Offices, and he shall have Power to Grant Reprieves and Pardons for Offenses against the United States, except in Cases of Impeachment.

He shall have Power, by and with the Advice and Consent of the Senate, to make Treaties, provided two-thirds of the Senators present concur; and he shall nominate, and by and with the Advice and Consent of the Senate, shall appoint Ambassadors, other public Ministers and Consuls, Judges of the supreme Court, and all other Officers of the United States, whose Appointments are not herein otherwise provided for, and which shall be established by Law: but the Congress may by Law vest the Appointment of such inferior Offices, as they think proper, in the President alone, in the Courts of Law, or in the Heads of Departments.

The President shall have Power to fill up all Vacancies that may happen during the Recess of the Senate by granting Commissions which shall expire at the End of their next Session.

Section 3.   He shall from time to time give to the Congress Information of the State of the Union, and recommend to their Consideration such Measures as he shall judge necessary and expedient; he may, on extraordinary Occasions, convene both Houses, or either of them, and in Cases of Disagreement between them, with Respect to the Time of Adjournment, he may adjourn them to such Time as he shall think proper; he shall receive Ambassadors and other public Ministers; he shall take Care that the Laws be faithfully executed, and shall Commission all of the Officers of the United States.

Section 4.   The President, Vice President and all civil Officers of the United States, shall be removed from Office on Impeachment for, and Conviction of, Treason, Bribery, or other high Crimes and Misdemeanors.

ARTICLE III

·   *Section 1.*   The judicial Power of the United States shall be vested in one supreme Court, and in such inferior Courts as the Congress may from time to time ordain and establish. The judges, both of the supreme and inferior Courts, shall hold their offices during good Behavior, and shall, at stated Times, receive for the Services a Compensation which shall not be diminished during their Continuance in Office.

Section 2. The judicial Power shall extend to all Cases, in Law and Equity, arising under this Constitution, the Laws of the United States and Treaties made, or which shall be made, under the Authority;–to all Cases affecting Ambassadors, other public Ministers and Consuls;–to all Cases of admiralty and maritime Jurisdiction;–to Controversies to which the United States shall be a Party;–to Controversies between two or more States;–between a State and Citizens of another State;[1]–Between Citizens of different States;–between Citizens of the same State claiming Lands under Grants of different States, and between a State, or the Citizens thereof, and foreign States, Citizens or Subjects.

In all Cases affecting Ambassadors, other public Ministers and Consuls, and those in which a State shall be a Party, the supreme Court shall have original Jurisdiction. In all the other Cases before mentioned, the supreme Court shall have appellate Jurisdiction, both as to Law and Fact, with such Exceptions, and under such Regulations as the Congress shall make.

The trial of all Crimes, except in Cases of Impeachment, shall be by Jury, and such Trial shall be held in the State where the said Crimes shall have been committed; but when not commited within any State, the Trial shall be at such Place or Places as the Congress may by Law have directed.

Section 3. Treason against the United States, shall consist only in levying War against them, or in adhering to their Enemies, giving them Aid and Comfort. No Person shall be convicted of Treason unless on the Testimony of two Witnesses to the same overt Act, or on Confession in open Court.

The Congress shall have power to declare the Punishment of Treason, but no Attainder of Treason shall work Corruption of Blood, or Forfeiture except during the Life of the Person attainted.

ARTICLE IV

Section 1. Full Faith and Credit shall be given in each State to the public acts, Records, and judicial Proceedings of every

---

[1] See the Eleventh Amendment.

other State. And the Congress may by general Laws prescribe the Manner in which such Acts, Records and Proceedings shall be proved, and the Effect thereof.

Section 2.   The Citizens of each State shall be entitled to all Privileges and Immunities of Citizens in the several States.

A Person charged in any State with Treason, Felony, or other Crime, who shall flee from Justice, and be found in another State, shall on demand of the executive Authority of the State from which he fled, be delivered up, to be removed to the State having Jurisdiction of the Crime.

No Person held to Service or Labour in one State, under the Laws thereof, escaping into another, shall in Consequence of any Law or Regulation therein, be discharged from such Service or Labour, but shall be delivered up on Claim of the Party to whom such Service or Labour may be due.[1]

Section 3.   New States may be admitted by the Congress into this Union; but no new States shall be formed or erected within the Jurisdiction of any other State; nor any State be formed by the Junction of two or more States, or parts of States, without the Consent of the Legislatures of the States concerned as well as of the Congress.

The Congress shall have Power to dispose of and make all needful Rules and Regulations respecting the Territory or other Property belonging to the United States; and nothing in this Constitution shall be so constructed as to Prejudice any Claims of the United States, or of any particular State.

Section 4.   The United States shall guarantee to every State in this Union of Republican Form of Government, and shall protect each of them against Invasion; and on Application of the Legislature, or of the Executive (when the Legislature cannot be convened) against domestic Violence.

ARTICLE V

The Congress whenever two-thirds of both houses shall deem it necessary, shall propose Amendments to this Constitution, or, on the Application of the Legislatures of two-thirds of the several States, shall call a Convention for proposing Amendments, which, in either Case, shall be valid to all Intents and Purposes, as

[1]   Obsolete. See the Thirteenth Amendment.

part of this Constitution, when ratified by the Legislature of three-fourths of the several States, or by Conventions in three-fourths thereof, as the one or the other Mode of Ratification may be proposed by the Congress; Provided that no Amendment which may be made prior to the Year One thousand eight hundred and eight shall in any Manner affect the first and fourth Clauses in the Ninth Section of the first Article; and that no State, without its Consent, shall be deprived of its equal Suffrage in the Senate.

ARTICLE VI

All Debts contracted and Engagements entered into, before the Adoption of this Constitution, shall be as valid against the United States under this Constitution, as under the Confederation.

This Constitution, and the Laws of the United States which shall be make in Purusance thereof; and all Treaties made, or which shall be made, under the Authority of the United States, shall be the supreme Law of the Land; and the Judges in every State shall be bound thereby, any Thing in the Constitution of Laws of any State to the Contrary notwithstanding.

The Senators and Representatives before mentioned, and the Members of the several State Legislatures, and all executive and judicial Officers, both of the United States and of the several States, shall be bound by Oath or Affirmation, to support this Constitution; but no religious Test shall ever be required as a Qualification to any Office or public Trust under the United States.

ARTICLE VII

The Ratification of the Conventions of nine States shall be sufficient for the Establishment of this Constitution between the States so ratifying the Same. Done in Convention by the Unanimous Consent of the States Present the Seventeenth Day of September in the Year of our Lord one thousand seven hundred and Eighty seven and of the Independence of the United States of America the Twelfth. In Witness whereof We have hereunto subscribed our Names.

Go. Washington
Presid't and deputy from Virginia

Delaware
Geo: Read
John Dickinson
Jaco: Broom
Gunning Bedford jun
Richard Bassett

Maryland
James McHenry
Danl Carroll
Dan: of St. Thos Jenifer

South Carolina
J. Rutledge
Charles Pinckney
Charles Cotesworth Pinckney
Pierce Butler

Georgia
William Few
Abr Baldwin

Virginia
John Blair
James Madison, Jr.

North Carolina
Wm Blount
Hu Williamson
Richd Dobbs Spaight

Pennsylvania
B. Franklin

New York
Alexander Hamilton

New Jersey
Wil: Livingston
David Brearley
Wm. Paterson
Jona: Dayton

New Hampshire
John Langdon
Nicholas Gilman

Massachusetts
Nathaniel Gorham
Rufus King

Connecticut
Wm. Saml Johnson
Roger Sherman
Robt. Morris

Thos. Fitzsimmons
James Wilson
Thomas Mifflin
Geo. Clymer
Jared Ingersoll
Gouv Morris

Attest:
William Jackson, Secretary

AMENDMENTS[1]

Amendment I

Congress shall make no law respecting an establishment of religion, or prohibiting the free exercise thereof; or abridging the freedom of speech, or of the press; or the right of the people peaceably to assemble, and to petition the Government for a redress of grievances.

Amendment II

A well regulated Militia, being necessary to the security of a free State, the right of the people to keep and bear Arms, shall not be infringed.

Amendment III

No Soldier shall, in time of peace be quartered in any house, without the consent of the Owner, nor in time of war, but in a manner to be prescribed by law.

Amendment IV

The right of the people to be secure in their persons, houses, papers, and effects, against unreasonable searches and seizures, shall not be violated, and no Warrants shall issue, but upon probable cause, supported by Oath or affirmation, and particularly describing the place to be searched, and the persons or things to be seized.

Amendment V

No person shall be held to answer for a capital, or otherwise infamous crime, unless on a presentment or indictment of a Grand Jury, except in cases arising in the land or naval forces, or in the Militia, when in actual service in time of War or public danger; nor shall any person be subject for the same offense to be twice put in jeopardy of life or limb, nor shall be compelled in any criminal case to be a witness against himself, nor be deprived of life, liberty, or property, without due process of law; nor shall private property be taken for public use, without just compensation.

[1] The first 10 Amendments were adopted in 1791.

Amendment VI

In all criminal prosecutions, the accused shall enjoy the right to a speedy and public trial, by an impartial jury of the State and district wherein the crime shall have been committed, which district shall have been previously ascertained by law, and to be informed of the nature and the cause of the accusation; to be confronted with the witnesses against him; to have the compulsory process for obtaining witnesses in his favor, and to have the Assistance of Counsel for his defense.

Amendment VII

In suits at common law, where the value in controversy shall exceed twenty dollars, the right of trial by jury shall be preserved, and no fact by a jury, shall be otherwise reexamined in any Court of the United States, than according to the rules of the common law.

Amendment VIII

Excessive bail shall not be required, nor excessive fines imposed, nor cruel and unusual punishments inflicted.

Amendment IV

The enumeration in the Constitution, of certain rights shall not be construed to deny or disparge others retained by the people.

Amendment X

The powers not delegated to the United States by the Constitution, nor prohibited by it to the States, are reserved to the States respectively, or to the people

Amendment XI[1]

The Judicial power of the United States shall not be construed to extend to any suit in law or equity, commenced or prosecuted against one of the United States by Citizens of another State, or by Citizens or Subjects of any Foreign States.

Amendment XII[2]

The Electors shall meet in their respective states and vote by ballot for President and Vice President, one of whom, at least,

[1] Adopted in 1798.
[2] Adopted in 1804.

shall not be inhabitant of the same state with themselves; they shall name in their ballots the person voted for as President and in distinct ballots the person voted for as Vice President, and they shall make distinct lists of all persons voted for as President, and of all persons voted for as Vice President, and of the number of votes for each, which lists they shall sign and certify, and transmit sealed to the seat of the government of the United States, directed to the President of the Senate;–The President of the Senate shall, in the presence of the Senate and House of Representatives, open all the certificates and the votes shall then be counted;–The person having the greatest number of votes for President, shall be the President, if such number be a majority of the whole number of Electors appointed; and if no person have such majority, then from the persons having the highest numbers not exceeding three on the list of those voted for as President, the House of Representatives shall choose immediately, by ballot, the President. But in choosing the President, the votes shall be taken by states, the representation from each state having one vote; a quorum for this purpose shall consist of a member or members from two-thirds of the states, and a majority of all the states shall be necessary to a choice. And if the House of Representatives shall not choose a President whenever the right of choice shall devolve upon them, before the fourth day of March next following, then the Vice President shall act as President, as in the case of the death or other constitutional disability of the President.–The person having the greatest number of votes as Vice President, shall be the Vice President, if such number be a majority of the whole number of Electors appointed, and if no person have a majority, then from the two highest numbers on the list, the Senate shall choose the Vice President; a quorum for the purpose shall consist of two-thirds of the whole number of Senators, and a majority of the whole number shall be necessary to a choice. But no person constitutionally ineligible to the office of President shall be eligible to that of Vice President of the United States.

Amendment XIII[1]

Section 1.   Neither slavery nor involuntary servitude, except as a punishment for crime whereof the party shall have been duly

[1] Adopted in 1865.

convicted, shall exist within the United States, or any place subject to their jurisdiction.

Section 2. Congress shall have power to enforce this article by appropriate legislation.

Amendment XIV[1]

Section 1. All persons born or naturalized in the United States and subject to the jurisdiction thereof, are citizens of the United States and of the State wherein they reside. No State shall make or enforce any law which shall abridge the privileges or immunities of citizens of the United States; nor shall any State deprive any person of life, liberty, or property, without the due process of law; nor deny to any person within its jurisdiction the equal protection of the laws.

Section 2. Representatives shall be apportioned among the several States according to their respective numbers, counting the whole number of persons in each State, excluding Indians not taxed. But when the right to vote at any election for the choice of electors for President and Vice President of the United States, Representatives in Congress, the Executive and Judicial Officers of a State, or the members of the Legislature thereof, is denied to any of the male inhabitants of such State, being twenty-one years of age, and citizens of the United States, or in any way abridged, except for participation in rebellion, or other crime, the basis of representation therein shall be reduced in the proportion which the number of such male citizens shall bear to the whole number of male citizens twenty-one years of age in such State.

Section 3. No person shall be Senator or Representative in Congress, or elector of President and Vice President, or hold any office, civil or military, under the United States, or under any State, who, having previously taken an oath, as a member of Congress, or as an officer of the United States, or as a member of any State legislature, or as an executive or judicial officer of any State, to support the Constitution of the United States, shall have engaged in insurrection or rebellion against the same, or given aid or comfort to the enemies thereof. But Congress may by a vote of two-thirds of each House, remove such disability.

Section 4. The validity of the public debt of the United States, authorized by law, including debts incurred for payment of

[1] Adopted in 1868.

pensions and bounties for services in suppressing insurrection or rebellion, shall not be questioned. But neither the United States nor any State shall assume or pay any debt or obligation incurred in aid or insurrection of rebellion against the United States, or any claim for the loss or emancipation of any slave; but all such debts, obligations and claims shall be held illegal and void.

Section 5. The Congress shall have power to enforce, by appropriate legislation, the provisions of this article.

Amendment XV[1]

Section 1. The right of citizens of the United States to vote shall not be denied or abridged by the United States or by any State on account of race, color, or previous condition of servitude.

Section 2. The Congress shall have power to enforce this article by appropriate legislation.

Amendment XVI[2]

The Congress shall have power to lay and collect taxes on incomes, from whatever source derived, without apportionment among the several States, and without regard to any census or enumeration.

Amendment XVII[3]

The Senate of the United States shall be composed of two Senators from each State, elected by the people thereof, for six years, and each Senator shall have one vote. The electors in each state shall have the qualifications requisite for electors of the most numerous branch of the state legislatures.

When vacancies happen in the representation of any State in the Senate, the executive authority of such State shall issue writs of election to fill such vacancies: Provided, That the legislature of any State may empower the executive thereof to make temporary appointments until the people fill the vacancies by election as the legislature may direct.

This amendment shall not be so construed as to affect the election of term of any Senator chosen before it becomes valid as part of the Constitution.

[1] Adopted in 1870.
[2] Adopted in 1913.
[3] Adopted in 1913.

Amendment XVIII[1]

Section 1.   After one year from the ratification of this article the manufacture, sale, or transportation in intoxicating liquors within, the importation thereof into, or the exportation thereof from the United States and all territory subject to the jurisdiction thereof for beverage purposes is hereby prohibited.

Section 2.   The Congress and the several States shall have concurrent power to enforce this article by appropriate legislation.

Section 3.   This article shall be inoperative unless it shall have been ratified as an amendment to the Constitution by the legislatures of the several States, as provided in the Constitution, within seven years from the date of the submission hereof to the States by the Congress.

Amendment XIX[2]

The right of Citizens of the United States to vote shall not be denied or abridged by the United States or by any State on account of sex.

Congress shall have power to enforce this article by appropriate legislation.

Amendment XX[3]

Section 1.   The terms of the President and Vice President shall end at noon on the 20th day of January, and the terms of Senators and Representatives at noon on the 3d day of January, of the years in which such terms would have ended if this article had not been ratified; and the terms of their successors shall then begin.

Section 2.   The Congress shall assemble at least once in every year, and such meeting shall begin at noon on the 3d day of January, unless they shall by law appoint a different day.

Section 3.   If, at the time fixed for the beginning of the term of the President, the President elect shall have died, the Vice President elect shall become President. If a President shall not have been chosen before the time fixed for the beginning of his term, or if the President elect shall have failed to qualify, then the Vice President elect shall act as President until a President shall

---

[1]   Adopted in 1919. Repealed by the Twenty-first Amendment.
[2]   Adopted in 1920.
[3]   Adopted in 1933.

have qualified; and the Congress may by law provide for the case wherein neither a President elect nor a Vice President elect shall have qualified, declaring who shall then act as President, or the manner in which one who is to act shall be selected, and such person shall act accordingly until President or Vice President shall have qualified.

Section 4. The Congress may by law provide for the case of the death of any of the persons from whom the House of Representatives may choose a President whenever the right of choice shall have devolved upon them, and for the case of the death of any of the persons from whom the Senate may choose a Vice President whenever the right of choice shall have devolved upon them.

Section 5. Sections 1 and 2 shall take effect on the 15th day of October following the ratification of this article.

Section 6. This article shall be inoperative unless it shall have been ratified as an amendment to the Constitution by the legislatures of three-fourths of the several States within seven years from the date of its submission.

Amendment XXI[1]

Section 1. The eighteenth article of amendment to the Constitution of the United States is hereby repealed.

Section 2. The transportation or importation into any State, Territory, or possession of the United States for delivery or use therein of intoxicating liquors, in violation of the laws thereof, is hereby prohibited.

Section 3. This article shall be inoperative unless it shall have been ratified as an amendment to the Constitution by conventions in the several States, as provided in the Constitution, within seven years from the date of the submission hereof to the States by the Congress.

Amendment XXII[2]

Section 1. No person shall be elected to the office of the President more than twice, and no person who has held the office of President, or acted as President, for more than two years of a term to which some other person was elected President shall be

[1] Adopted in 1933.
[2] Adopted in 1951.

elected to the office of the President more than once. But this Article shall not apply to any person holding the office of President when this Article was proposed by the Congress, and shall not prevent any person who may be holding the office of President, or acting as President, during the term within which this Article becomes operative from holding the office of President or acting as President during the remainder of such term.

Section 2.   This article shall be inoperative unless it shall have been ratified as an amendment to the Constitution by the Legislatures of three-fourths of the several States within seven years from the date of its submission to the States by the Congress.

Amendment XXIII[1]

Section 1.   The District constituting the seat of Government of the United States shall appoint in such manner as the Congress may direct:

A number of electors of President and Vice President equal to the whole number of Senators and Representatives in Congress to which the District would be entitled if it were a State, but in no event more than the least populous State; they shall be in addition to those appointed by the States; but they shall be considered, for the purposes of the election of President and Vice President, to be electors appointed by a State; and they shall meet in the District and perform such duties as provided by the twelfth article of amendment.

Section 2.   The Congress shall have power to enforce this article by appropriate legislation.

Amendment XXIV[2]

Section 1.   The right of citizens of the United States to vote in any primary or other election for the President or Vice President, for electors for President or Vice President, or for Senator or Representative in Congress, shall not be denied or abridged by the United States or any State by reason of failure to pay any poll tax or other tax.

Section 2.   The Congress shall have power to enforce this article by appropriate legislation.

[1]   Adopted in 1961.
[2]   Adopted in 1964.

Amendment XXV[1]

Section 1.   In case of the removal of the President from office or his death or resignation, the Vice President shall become President.

Section 2.   Whenever there is a vacancy in the office of the Vice President, the President shall nominate a Vice President who shall take the office upon confirmation by a majority vote of both houses of Congress.

Section 3.   Whenever the President transmits to the President pro tempore of the Senate and the Speaker of the House of Representatives his written declaration that he is unable to discharge the powers and duties of his office, and until he transmits to them a written declaration to the contrary, such powers and duties shall be discharged by the Vice President as Acting President.

Section 4.   Whenever the Vice President and a majority of either the principal officers of the executive departments or of such other body as Congress may by law provide, transmit to the President pro tempore of the Senate and the Speaker of the House of Representatives their written declaration that the President is unable to discharge the powers and duties of his office, the Vice President shall immediately assume the powers and duties of the office as Acting President.

Thereafter, when the President transmits to the President pro tempore of the Senate and the Speaker of the House of Representatives, his written declaration that no inability exists, he shall resume the powers and duties of his office unless the Vice President and a majority of either the principal officers of the executive department or of such other body as Congress may by law provide, transmit within four days to the President pro tempore of the Senate and the Speaker of the House of Representatives their written declaration that the President is unable to discharge the powers and duties of his office. Thereupon Congress shall decide the issue, assembling within 48 hours for that purpose if not in session. If the Congress, within 21 days after receipt of the latter written declaration, or, if Congress is not in session, with 21 days after Congress is required to assemble, determines by two-thirds vote of both houses that the President is unable to discharge the powers and duties of his office, the Vice

[1]   Adopted in 1967.

President shall continue to discharge the same as Acting President; otherwise, the President shall resume the powers and duties of his office.

Amendment XXVI[1]

Section 1. The Right to Citizens of the United States, who are eighteen years of age or older, to vote shall not be denied or abridged by the United States or by any State on account of age.

Section 2. The Congress shall have power to enforce this article by appropriate legislation.

Proposed Amendment XXVII[2]

Section 1. Equality of rights under the law shall not be denied or abridged by the United States or by any State on account of sex.

Section 2. The Congress shall have the power to enforce, by appropriate legislation, the provisions of this article.

Section 3. This amendment shall take effect two years after the date of ratification.

[1] Adopted in 1971.
[2] Proposed March 22, 1972.

GLOSSARY

Abscam: A scandal in the 1970s where FBI agents posing as Arab sheikhs entrapped various government officials for violating federal law by commiting fraud against the United States.

Appropriation bill: An appropriation bill grants the money to be made available for an authorisation bill, and this may be less than the total permissible in the authorisation bill. Appropriation bills originate in the House of Representatives, and are considered by the House and Senate Appropriations Committees after the Budget Committees have agreed on the ceiling or limit of possible appropriations for particular sections of the budget. Bills concerned with raising money, i.e., taxation, are dealt with in Congress by the House Ways and Means and the Senate Finance Committee. All committee decisions are approved, amended or rejected by the House and Senate as a whole.

Authorisation bill: Most legislative proposals come before Congress in the form of bills. An authorisation bill authorises a programme, indicates its general objectives and often puts a ceiling on the amount of money to be used to finance it.

Bill of Rights: The first ten Amendments to the US Constitution. Certain individual rights or guarantees against the actions of the national government are specified. These include freedom of speech and assembly. No person can be deprived of life, liberty, or property without due process of law. The Fourteenth Amendment specifies certain individual rights against state governments. For example, no state shall deprive any person of life, liberty, or property without due process of law, nor deny any person within its jurisdiction the equal protection of the laws.

Caucus: A closed meeting of party members to selected party candidates or national party convention delegates. The term is also used to describe the private party meetings of elected legislators.

Executive privilege: A term coined in 1958 to justify the claim that the President had the constitutional authority to withhold information from the Congress and the courts. This claim has never been accepted by the Congress, and in 1974 in *United States* v. *Nixon* the Supreme Court rejected President Nixon's claim of executive privilege with respect to tapes of conservations between himself and his White House aides.

Federalism: A system of government where power is divided between national or central government and regional or state governments. Both governments act directly on the people, and both are supreme within their own sphere of authority, and have specified powers. By contrast, a *unitary* system of government is one where the national government is supreme, and local governments derive their authority from the national government, and exercise only those powers given to them by the national government.

In the United States, the Constitution (according to Article VI) is the supreme law of the land, while the basic principle of federalism is set out in the *Tenth Amendment*, which states that the government possesses those powers delegated in the Constitution, and all other powers are reserved to the states. Local governments, such as cities and counties, have a *unitary* relationship with state governments, except in some states whose constitutions permit the state governments to grant 'home rule' to localities.

Fiscal policy: The use of public revenue or governmental financial policies and programmes to influence the national economy. Such policies might include public works legislation, tax reductions or increases, reductions in government spending or incurring a budget deficit. The use of governmental fiscal policies to effect changes in the economy is reflected in the national budget which is drawn up within the executive branch, but it is Congress which makes the final decisions on the specific detail of the budget annually.

General Accounting Office: An independent agency which acts as an agent of Congress. The GAO conducts financial audits of government departments, checking that the expenditure of money conforms to the intent of Congress.

GOP: 'Grand Old Party', the nickname of the Republican Party.

Hearing: Hearings are held by committees or sub-committees of Congress to obtain information on proposed bills, or to check on the implementation of legislation by agencies and departments. Individual citizens, representatives of interest groups, other members of Congress, and agency or department heads and officials, are all permitted to testify at such hearings.

Non-partisan elections: Elections where candidates have not party designations and where political parties are normally prohibited from running candidates. States such as Nebraska have a strong tradition of non-partisanship which extends to elections for the one-house state legislature. The movement to bar the use of political party labels on the ballot was one of the reforms initiated early in this century, and was linked to the council-manager form of local government. Some city mayors are also elected in non- partisan elections, notably Newark, New Jersey.

Political action committees: Organisations or auxiliaries formed originally by business and trade union groups to collect money to be used for political campaigns in support of candidates in elections. In recent years they have been joined by 'ideological' committees representing a broad range of interests, or single issues – examples include the National Committee for an Effective Congress (NCEC), the National Conservative Political Action Committee (NCPAC), or the National Rifle Association Political Action Committee. In 1980 an important conservative force was the religious organisation, the Moral Majority, Inc.

Primary elections: These elections take place *within* the political parties, and there are several types. The *direct primary* is an intra-party election where voters select the candidates who will be the nominees of the party in the subsequent general election. Primaries are also used to select delegates to the national party conventions. In a *closed primary*, the selection process is limited to registered party members. In an *open primary*, voters can participate regardless of party affiliation. Candidates are normally put on the primary election ballot as a result of petitions signed by a required number of registered voters. All states use direct primaries of some type for some elected offices, and in recent presidential election years a majority of states have held some form of primary elections prior to the two major national party conventions where the presidential and vice-presidential candidates are chosen.

Propositions: An electoral device, whereby citizens can propose legislation or constitutional amendments through initiatives or petitions signed by a required number of registered voters. The number of signatories varies in different states. The proposition appears on the ballot at election time and is voted on by the electorate. If a proposition secures a majority of those voting then it is binding on the elected branches of the state government. Such propositions have been used in states such as California to force the government to make financial economies, or lower certain taxes.

Seniority system: A system or procedure in both Houses of Congress whereby committee chairmanships are given to the majority party member with the longest continuous service on the committee. Both parties list their members on the different committees according to this principle of seniority. Strict or automatic application of this system by the parties in Congress was eroded in the 1970s.

Split-ticket voting: A term used to describe what happens when a voter switches parties when choosing candidates for different offices on the ballot, e.g., one voter may vote for a Republican presidential candidate while for the congressional elections vote for a Democrat.

Vice-President: The elected official who presides over the Senate, and who assumes the presidency following the death, resignation, removal or disability of the President. Elected on the same ballot as the President. Under the terms of the *25th Amendment*, passed in 1967, when there is a vacancy in the office of Vice-President the President nominates a Vice-President who is confirmed by a majority vote of both Houses of Congress. Gerald Ford was so chosen in 1973, and in August 1974 assumed the presidency on the resignation of Richard Nixon. The first non-elected President, Ford nominated Nelson Rockefeller as Vice-President, and after confirmation he served until 1977. In the event of presidential disability the Vice-President becomes Acting President.

INDEX